CULTURES OF THE WORLD
Ghana

Cavendish
Square
New York

Published in 2019 by Cavendish Square Publishing, LLC
243 5th Avenue, Suite 136, New York, NY 10016

Copyright © 2019 by Cavendish Square Publishing, LLC

Third Edition

Library of Congress Cataloging-in-Publication Data
Names: Robinson, Peg, author. | Levy, Patricia, 1951- author. | Wong, Winnie, author.
Title: Ghana / Peg Robinson, Patricia Levy, and Winnie Wong.
Description: First edition. | New York : Cavendish Square, 2018. | Series: Cultures of the world | Includes bibliographical references and index.
Identifiers: LCCN 2018028757 (print) | LCCN 2018032297 (ebook) | ISBN 9781502640734 (ebook) | ISBN 9781502640727 (library bound)
Subjects: LCSH: Ghana--Juvenile literature.
Classification: LCC DT510 (ebook) | LCC DT510 .R56 2018 (print) | DDC 966.7--dc23
LC record available at https://lccn.loc.gov/2018028757

Editorial Director: David McNamara
Editor: Elizabeth Schmermund
Copy Editor: Nathan Heidelberger
Associate Art Director: Alan Sliwinski
Designer: Jessica Nevins
Production Coordinator: Karol Szymczuk
Photo Research: J8 Media

Printed in the United States of America

CONTENTS

GHANA TODAY

THE NATION KNOWN AS GHANA WAS FORMED IN 1957. IT LIES ON the southwestern shore of northern Africa, in territory long famous for its wealth of resources, and takes its name from a kingdom that once flourished to the north of the modern state. It was the first sub-Saharan African nation to regain independence after European colonization.

European contact within Ghana began as early as 1471, when Portuguese traders came looking for gold and ivory. The nation's history is marked by the European forts that serve as landmarks, illustrating the drama of centuries of exploitation, colonization, trade, slavery, and wars, both foreign and domestic.

In 1957, after centuries of disruption during the slave trade and colonial periods, the nation at last gained independence and self-government. The new state of Ghana suffered a long series of tyrannies and unrest before finally returning to a democratic, multiparty government in 1992. It is currently considered to be among the most stable of African nations. With its vast natural resources, a peaceful political climate, and premium education for its people, Ghana is set to become a leading African nation in the twenty-first century.

This change is a dramatic tale of success, pointing to a future much of Africa still struggles to match. Ghana was the preeminent slave source during the period from roughly 1500 to 1850, when the British began to establish themselves as the colonial power in the region, and it suffered all the cultural chaos associated with the slave trade. The situation after colonization was generally more peaceful, but equally traumatic. To gain freedom took struggle. To have that freedom succeed is a glorious victory.

The benefits of that victory support Ghana in its current form. It is a stable country, with very limited violence over the past twenty years. This peace provides a welcome basis for domestic production, for foreign investment, and for foreign trade. It allows Ghanaian businesses, both small and large, to expand, developing a deeper and more securely rooted economy than many nations can offer. Its peace and prosperity allow an ever-increasing portion of its population to gain education, from the compulsory education provided until at least age fifteen to increasingly competitive access to higher levels of education. Ghana can provide a population of trained, skilled workers, most speaking at least some level of English, available to meet the demands of an international market. Ghana's resources, from nonrenewable gold to renewable cola and forest products, bring in annual profits that sustain progress.

All these elements illustrate why Ghana draws in a steady tourist trade, both those looking for the history and culture and those who desire a new, safe vacation site, with beautiful beaches, interesting attractions, high standards, and reliable communication through the lingua franca of English, the national language shared to varying degrees by all groups.

Ghana offers this and more. It is a lively, multicultural society, drawing from over fifty different ethnic groups. Its primary tribal populations are the Akan, Dagomba, and Ewe tribal families. Other groups are less strongly represented. Immigrant groups, including Chinese, have been a cause of tension in the country, leading to ongoing efforts to remove and limit immigration in an attempt to preserve Ghana's resources and its jobs. The region has been repeatedly taken advantage of, and modern leaders and their people are determined to retain Ghana's comparative economic stability and build upon it in years to come.

Ghana remains strongly influenced by English and European culture, offering a familiar setting for many guests. Ghanaian businesses and hosts appreciate the benefits brought by tourists and by international business. The arts, culture, and cuisine of the country's many regional and tribal groups combine the familiar, the unexpected, and the challenging—an enticing blend for those visiting for recreational or business reasons. City life presents a great array of performers, musicians, and artists. There are restaurants, hotels, clubs, theaters, galleries,

Cape Coast Castle remains an important tourist site today.

and all the recreational activities to be expected of a tourist destination. Further outside the urban areas, the countryside is socially stable, with a growing infrastructure and bountiful resources.

Ghana has proven to be a secure African state, willing to fight for the ideals they claimed when demanding independence. Their government has survived several crises, successfully and peacefully transferred power between opposing parties, and maintained civil order for well over two decades. To many, it is a model African nation, with roots in the past while great prospects for the future are being developed in the investments of the present. Its people take pride in their nation and welcome visitors from other lands.

Those planning a visit should prepare for a tropical equatorial climate. The southern coastal areas are subject to ocean influences, with high humidity and higher precipitation. There is a strong beach culture, including surfing, and beaches are a favored local getaway. Coastal cities support a small fishing community and display the remaining landmarks of the slaving and the colonial eras, in particular the slave forts. Cape Coast is the key coastal city, providing a hospitable destination for tourists. Tema is a major port, with shipping and local manufacture. Accra, the nation's capital, is also on the coast. It is the central location for those seeking contact with major businesses, governmental officials, and educational institutes, and it is the heart of Ghana's cultural activities.

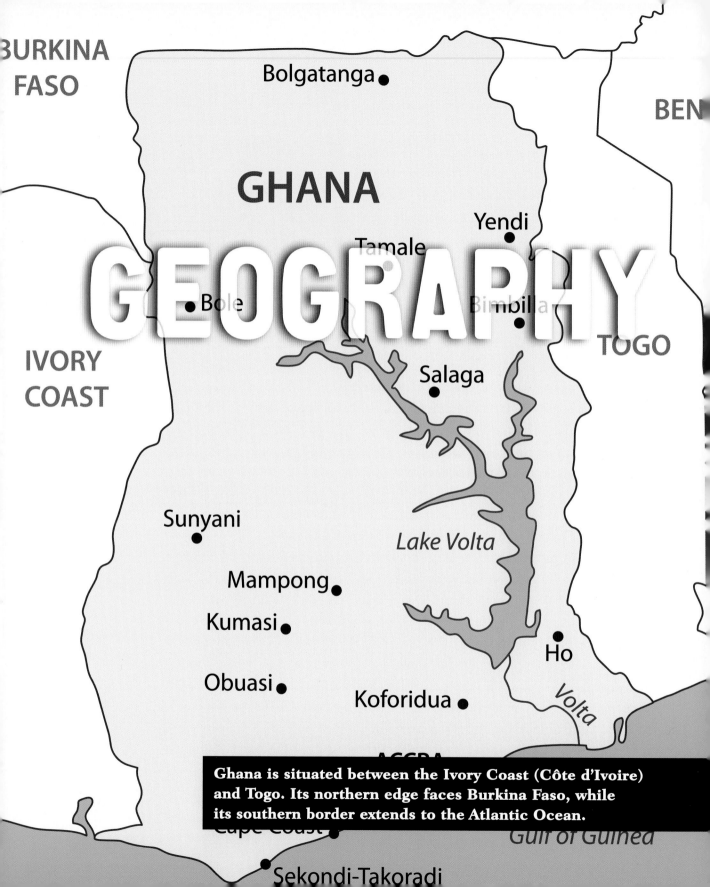

BURKINA
FASO

BEN

GHANA

IVORY
COAST

TOGO

Bolgatanga •

Yendi •

Tamale

Bole •

Bimbila •

Salaga •

Lake Volta

Sunyani •

Mampong •

Kumasi •

Ho •

Obuasi •

Koforidua •

Volta

ACCRA

Ghana is situated between the Ivory Coast (Côte d'Ivoire) and Togo. Its northern edge faces Burkina Faso, while its southern border extends to the Atlantic Ocean.

Cape Coast •

Gulf of Guinea

Sekondi-Takoradi •

GHANA LIES ON THE GOLD AND IVORY Coast of Africa—the south-facing western coast extending out into the Atlantic on the Gulf of Guinea. Its coastline is 335 miles (539 kilometers) long. The majority of its cities lie along the coast, including the nation's capital, Accra, and its major port, Tema. The nation is 92,098 square miles (238,533 square kilometers) in area, with one major central river, the Volta, running from north to south.

Ghana is bounded to the east by Togo, to the north by Burkina Faso, and to the west by Côte d'Ivoire (the Ivory Coast). It can be divided into four approximate regions: the coastal plain to the far south, the forest-dissected plateau in the central eastern portion of the nation, the savanna high plains in the north and northwest, and the sandstone basin of the Volta region in the east.

Ghana, in the deep past, was once part of the supercontinent of Gondwanaland. During the Mesozoic period of separation, it drew away from the area of South America now known as Brazil. Later forces drove the land upward, creating the complex and mineral-rich land that is now modern Ghana.

In 2017, floods in low-lying Accra caused great disruption.

REGIONS

THE COASTAL PLAIN This long, low strip of sandy shore is intersected by several rivers and streams, most of which are navigable only by canoe. It stretches 50 miles (80 km) inland at its eastern and western ends, but narrows to around 10 miles (16 km) in the middle. Divided in half by the capital city of Accra, the coastal plain is low lying, with an average elevation of 246 feet (75 meters) above sea level. Some areas, such as the lagoon at Keta, are below sea level and occasionally flood.

THE FOREST-DISSECTED PLATEAU The plateau occupies a large triangular area of the southwest of Ghana, including part of the southern coast. The landscape is mostly gently rolling hills, with broad, flat valleys in between. The region consists of primary rain forest in the extreme southwest, with plantations of hardwood and cacao trees, which produce cocoa beans, making up the rest of the plateau.

THE SAVANNA HIGH PLAINS This inverted L-shaped band of land in the north and northwest of the country varies from 300 to 2,900 feet (91 to 884 m) above sea level and is made up of smoothly undulating plains dotted with occasional small, rounded hills. The land is dry and covered with tall grasses, some reaching 10 to 12 feet (3 to 3.7 m), low bushes, and the random tree. Because of the underlying rock that blocks draining, some parts are swampy. From November to March, no rain falls in this region, and the land dries out completely. Nevertheless, the plants survive, as they have adapted to withstand long periods of drought.

THE VOLTAIAN SANDSTONE BASIN This consists of about 43,540 square miles (112,770 sq km) of land in the eastern half of the country. Like the northwest, it is covered in savanna-like vegetation, but it is flatter and has a lower elevation, some 200 to 600 feet (60 to 180 m) above sea level. Around its edges rise several ridges and mountains.

To the east is the Akwapim-Togo range, which includes Mount Afadjato, at 2,903 feet (885 m) Ghana's highest point, while to the west is a long, narrow plateau. At its heart is the water system of Lake Volta.

THE WEATHER

Although close to the equator, Ghana has a moderate climate, with sunshine throughout the year. The southwest is hot and humid, while the east is warm and dry. In the north, temperatures during the dry season can reach 100 degrees Fahrenheit (38 degrees Celsius). Nowhere in Ghana do average temperatures fall below 77°F (25°C). The hottest time of the year in the south usually is April, just before the long wet season. The coldest is August, just after the wet season. All of Ghana experiences dry and wet seasons, but the effect of the dry season is less noticeable in the south. The coastal area and the forested areas have two wet seasons—a long season between April and July and a

Visitors enjoy the lush forests at Kakum National Park.

THE HARMATTAN

The harmattan is a wind that affects large areas of Africa. It originates in the Sahara and blows down across Ghana from the north and northeast. It is a hot, dry wind that carries a large amount of red dust, which is deposited throughout the country. The forested areas in the southwest of the country break up this wind and protect the southwest from its drying effect.

The harmattan can be devastating. In 1983, it blew across the entire country, disrupting the rainy season and causing a major drought that resulted in serious food shortages. Famine was narrowly avoided by the arrival of food donated by other countries.

shorter one from September to November. The north experiences only one wet season, between September and November.

The country, like its neighbors, is experiencing the first signs of climate change, however. Temperatures show signs of rising, there is increasing coastal erosion, and storms have increased in number and intensity, while proving hard to predict. The country is in the midst of attempting to plan for further changes, seeking ways to prepare their communities and adapt their agriculture and industry to cope with these problems.

PRECIPITATION

Ghana is affected by two large air masses—one flows northward from the southern Atlantic Ocean, while the other flows south from the Sahara Desert. The first is a humid, warm body of air that keeps day and night temperatures at around 77°F (25°C). The second is very dry and brings hot daytime temperatures, low nighttime temperatures, and clear skies.

Those two air masses effectively create regional weather conditions in Ghana. The extreme southwest of the country is the most influenced by the southern air mass. It receives about 75 inches (190 centimeters) of rain a year. As the air mass moves north, it loses water, so the northern part of the country receives much less rain. The Accra coastal plain has the lowest rainfall—from 40 inches (102 cm) a year to less than 30 inches (76 cm), with a current average of 33 inches (84 cm). In this region, the land is flat, so the unobstructed clouds drift by without releasing any water.

The Volta River

WATERWAYS

Ghana's river systems are fed by both rainfall and mountain springs. In the north of the country, seasonal rivers that receive only rainwater are either flooded during the rainy season or are completely parched in the dry season. Though water volume in spring-fed streams shrinks in the dry season, the streams do not dry up completely. In the forested zone, where rainfall is more consistent, the rivers flow throughout the year. In western Ghana, several small rivers cut across the coastal plain as they drain into the Gulf of Guinea. The Pra, the Ankobra, and the Tano are the largest of those permanent rivers, but they are barely navigable as they have many rapids and waterfalls.

Ghana has only one natural lake, Bosumtwi, in the south-central interior. About 19 square miles (49 sq km) in area, the lake is almost perfectly round and was formed in a meteorite impact crater. It is surrounded by high hills. Streams in the hills feed Bosumtwi, many of them flowing around the lake before spilling into it. There are also several ocean lagoons. The largest of them is the one at Keta in the southeast.

The Volta, Ghana's longest river, is fed by several major tributaries. The Black Volta rises in Burkina Faso, where it is called the Baoule. It travels along Ghana's border with Côte d'Ivoire and empties into the Volta. The White Volta also rises in Burkina Faso, but it flows almost due south to join the Volta. Both rivers are not navigable during the dry season, but they flood during

Lake Volta is among the world's largest artificial lakes, covering 3,275 square miles (8,482 sq km). Its dam at Akosombo stands 440 feet (134 m) high. In addition to generating electricity and providing inland waterway transportation, Lake Volta is potentially valuable for irrigation and fish farming.

The damming of the Volta in the 1960s turned much of the Volta River into Lake Volta.

the wet season. Two other tributaries, the Afram and the Oti, also feed the Volta River. The Oti rises in Burkina Faso, crosses Togo, and enters Ghana to join the Volta.

In the 1960s, the Volta was dammed near the town of Akosombo to create a hydroelectric power station. This turned much of the Volta River into Lake Volta. In operation by early 1966, the power station is about 2,200 feet (670 m) long. A smaller dam, at Kpong, was built farther south. The Black Volta also has been dammed at Bui, in the northwest of the country.

PLANTS AND ANIMALS

Ghana is a lowland country that has three types of vegetation, largely determined by rainfall and human activity. In the southwest is the tropical rain forest, where rainfall exceeds 65 inches (165 cm) annually. Farther east and north is a large band of deciduous forest.

Most of southern Ghana consists of evergreen and secondary forest—forestland that was once logged and cultivated, but which has since been reclaimed by the forest. Valuable African hardwoods such as mahogany, iroko (odum), and ebony are found there. Midway between deciduous forest and savanna, the region is the largest vegetation zone in Ghana, covering about 65,600 square miles (170,000 sq km). Trees found there include baobab, acacia, and shea trees. In the wet season, such vegetation becomes very green. Tall grasses, up to 12 feet (3.7 m) high, cover the ground, waving gently in the breeze. In the dry season, the trees lose their leaves and the grasses turn yellow.

The forest gradually gives way to the grasses and bushes of the savanna in the northern two-thirds of the country. The Black and the White Volta Rivers join to form the Volta, which runs south to the sea through a narrow gap in the hills.

In the southeast of the country, around Accra, is a stretch of coastal grassland of tall grass and scrub—stunted trees and bushes. This area receives little rain but is very humid. The few trees there include the drought- and fire-resistant baobab and nim, while in the wetter areas wild oil palms and fan palms grow.

In the dry savanna areas of Ghana, huge termite mounds can be found, which look like miniature mud palaces. The termite colonies actually live underground, while the tall towers of the mounds are built to funnel air into the nests.

THE BAOBAB TREE

The people of Ghana use the peculiar baobab tree in many ways. It grows throughout Africa in savanna areas and looks as if it has been turned upside down, with its branches buried in the soil and its roots sticking up in the air. The trunk can grow to a diameter of 30 feet (9 m) and as tall as 59 feet (18 m). Its mass of foliage can spread out to 150 feet (46 m) in diameter.

The fruit of the tree is large and gourd-like and can be eaten. The trunk is often hewn and hollowed out to make barrels used to collect and store rainwater. The bark can be made into rope and cloth, while the tree itself provides shade in many villages and is often the site of the village school.

Around the coastal lagoons and the Volta River, in the southeast, are mangrove swamps, where the vegetation has adapted to living in salt water. Mangrove trees grow to about 50 feet (15 m) and have tall aerial roots that help the plants remain upright in the soft mud of tidal waters.

Ghana has a rich and diverse animal life. Like the forests, however, that variety is seriously threatened because of the steadily encroaching human population. Ghana has over two hundred species of mammals, including elephants, leopards, wild buffalo, antelope, hyenas, wild pigs, and many kinds of primates. Once plentiful throughout the savanna, the elephants and lions are now rare and largely confined to nature reserves. Crocodiles and hippos are common along the rivers, and many species of poisonous snakes pose a danger to people. Cobras, puff adders, and horned

Elephants roam the Ghanaian savanna.

Elmina Castle is an important landmark along Ghana's southern coast.

adders can kill with their venomous bite, while pythons can squeeze their victims to death. More than 725 species of birds live in Ghana, from huge eagles to tiny swallows. Among the numerous birds are parrots, hornbills, kingfishers, herons, cuckoos, sunbirds, egrets, vultures, and snakebirds.

CITIES OF GHANA

ACCRA The capital city of Ghana since 1877, Accra has a population of 2.3 million. Located on the Gulf of Guinea, the Accra area was already the site of several tribal villages when Portuguese sailors arrived there in 1471. Colonized in the seventeenth century by the Dutch, English, and Danes in turn, it grew into a prosperous trading center, blending contemporary and traditional African customs and architecture.

The administrative and financial center of Ghana, Accra possesses luxury hotels, fine restaurants, and lively entertainment. The heritage of Ghana from prehistoric to modern times is on display in museums dating from colonial times, and further reflected in its cathedrals and other architectural landmarks. The University of Ghana at Legon, founded in 1948 in a suburb of Accra, showcases beautiful tropical gardens.

A soccer stadium and racecourse provide settings for sports, while Black Star Square is the center of cultural activities. On weekends, tourists and resident Ghanaians head for the beaches along the city's shores or take trains to beaches in other towns.

The main industries of Accra are food processing and the manufacture of textiles and lumber. Most of Ghana's imports arrive at Tema, 16 miles (26 km) to the east of the city, and are then transported to Accra to be distributed around the country.

Watching soccer is a favorite pastime not only in the capital city of Accra but across the entire country.

This historical fort is located in Kumasi, the largest city in Ghana.

Like many cities in Africa, Accra has a mix of rich and poor. The relatively well-off own houses, cars, and electrical appliances, while others live with few possessions, poor sanitation, and scant comforts in shantytowns around the dismal edges of the city.

KUMASI Kumasi has surpassed Accra as the largest city in Ghana, with a population of 2.6 million. Kumasi is located in south-central Ghana, about 125 miles (200 km) northwest of Accra. An ancient city, it was the seventeenth-century capital of the Ashanti (or Asante) Kingdom. Kumasi is situated at the junction of main roads and is the principal transit point for goods from the interior on their way to Accra and the seaports. This busy hub has teacher-training colleges, the University of Science and Technology, and agricultural research institutions.

The area around Kumasi is dedicated to cacao farming, which brings in much of the city's wealth. The Ashanti people, who still keep their capital at Kumasi, weave the colorful silk and cotton kente cloth, which is a profitable cottage industry. The city has an armed forces museum housed in an old British fort. It also has a cultural center. The largest market in all Ghana is spread out there, selling everything from handicrafts to auto parts. Traditional Ashanti buildings in Kumasi were designated a UNESCO World Heritage site in 1980.

OTHER TOWNS The major town in the north of Ghana is Tamale, with a population of over 370,000. It was developed as a town around 1907 when the British chose it as the administrative center of the northern region, a role it still holds. Other large towns in the north include Yendi and Bolgatanga, both built along main roads of the area. Bolgatanga is the most northerly major town of Ghana and has a population of about 66,600. It serves as an administrative center for the Frafra district.

Along the coast are a string of towns first established by European colonists, such as Sekondi-Takoradi, Cape Coast, Elmina, and Saltpond, with populations of 560,000 or less. A port city, Sekondi-Takoradi has an artificial harbor. It also has sawmills, paper factories, and an airport for light aircraft. Cape Coast is known as an educational center and has many schools and colleges as well as a university.

INTERNET LINKS

http://www.ghana.travel
The official Ghana tourism site offers travel tips and information about visiting the country.

https://www.worldatlas.com/af/gh/where-is-ghana.html
The World Atlas entry for Ghana features geographical information about the country.

HISTORY

Kwame Nkrumah was the first prime minister and president of Ghana.

2

BEFORE THE FIRST EUROPEANS EVEN reached the Gold and Ivory Coasts of Africa, the land encompassing West Africa was great. Between about 400 CE to 1240 CE, the Ghana Empire prospered, followed by the great Empire of Benin. The Ashanti established their own rule in what is now Ghana. Before the Europeans ever came, Ghana had cities and technology, trade and wealth.

Later, after the Europeans came, this land was known as the Gold Coast. It was known for slaves and for reserves of gold. After Europeans arrived, things were different. But for thousands of years, Ghana was just what it was: land and people, trees, animals, and tribes. Good food that is eaten to this day. Beautiful bronzes that are still created. Glorious gold used to enrich the beauty of objects. Wonderful stories that told of the mysterious, animistic connection between men and the world around them. The Ghana of today shows the scars of four hundred years of the slave trade and colonization, but Ghana's history is deep, and most of its culture comes from the millennia that happened before the Europeans came.

BEGINNINGS

Little is known about the early inhabitants of Ghana. Stone tools dating back to 5500—2500 BCE found in the plains around Accra suggest a hunter-gatherer community of people who lived by the sea and moved around, gathering berries and wild seeds and hunting animals. The oral traditions of some tribes in Ghana also reveal a little about their early history. For example, stories by the Ewe people, who live in the southeast of Ghana, say that they immigrated to Ghana around 1600 CE, after being driven out of modern Benin by another tribe. The Ga and Adangme, who live in the area around Accra, believe their ancestors came from southern Nigeria during the sixteenth century and conquered another tribe of people called the Guan. The Ga founded a small state called the Kingdom of Accra, whose capital was inland from the modern city.

The oral tradition of the inland Akan people tells that they first lived in Ghana around the thirteenth century, in the northwest grasslands. As the Akan Kingdom grew, groups migrated south to the forested areas and farther south to the coast.

TRADE ROUTES

Long before the arrival of Europeans to the west coast of Africa, those kingdoms traded with one another and with tribes from farther afield. The northwest trade route ran south from the ancient kingdom of Mali through modern Ghana and then south to modern Nigeria. From the busy trading town of Kumasi in central Ghana, more trade routes led to the coast. Along the trade routes came caravans carrying dates, salt, tobacco, and copper. The settlements of Ghana traded cloth, ostrich feathers, and tanned hides, as well as cola nuts and slaves.

After 1591, great changes took place in Ghana's trading patterns, setting the future course of its history. That year, war broke out between the Songhai Empire, Ghana's chief trading partner to the north, and the Moors of North Africa. As a result, the Songhai Empire fell into decline, bringing to a close the Ghanaian's trade with the north.

EUROPEAN CONTACT

More than a century earlier, in 1471, Portuguese traders had arrived near Elmina on the southwest coast. Their original intention was to find a sea route to the lucrative markets of the Far East, and they sailed along the coast of Africa searching for such a passage. Venturing ashore, they discovered that the local people wore gold jewelry. The traders reported that news back to their king, John II. In 1481, a special mission led by Diogo d'Azambuja was sent to Ghana. They found much gold and in 1482 built a fort at Elmina. Trade between Portugal and the tribes of Ghana flourished, with gold dominating the business. The Portuguese later built more forts—at Axim, Shama, and Accra—to store the gold while their trading ships were at sea and to protect the Portuguese traders and sailors from both the indigenous people and the English and Dutch, who were also exploring the area.

In 1598, the Dutch began building forts at Mouri, Butri, Kormantsi, and Komeda, all along the southern coast of Ghana. Fierce competition between the Dutch and Portuguese for control of the area persisted, and in 1637 and 1642 the Dutch captured two Portuguese forts. During the seventeenth century, the English, Germans, and Danes also built forts along the shore. Greedy for ivory and gold, they sailed in with shiploads of rum, cotton, beads, mirrors, guns, and gunpowder to exchange with the local people.

The European traders competed with one another for favor with the indigenous clans. They paid rent for their forts to the local chiefs and respected the chiefs' edicts that they not venture into the interior but remain in the coastal forts, where trade goods were brought to them. Occasionally the Europeans were expected to lend a hand in intertribal battles.

THE ASHANTI

When the Akan people first migrated into Ghana, some settled around the confluence of the Pra and Ofin Rivers. As their kingdom grew, some families moved north and founded the powerful Ashanti Empire, also called the Asante Empire, in the Kumasi area. During the seventeenth century, a tribal chief named Osei Tutu formed an alliance among the ethnic groups in the area.

Yaa Asantewaa (d. 1921), a queen of the Ashanti around the turn of the twentieth century, rallied her people during the British colonial era, resisting domination by foreign powers and the pillage of national treasures such as the Ashanti golden stool. The long battle was eventually lost, and Yaa Asantewaa was exiled to the Seychelles Islands. Her place in Ghanaian history and her people's respect, however, has never been lost.

The following is her most famous speech, given to rally her men and women to battle:

Now, I see that some of you fear to go forward to fight for our king. If it was in the brave days of Osei Tutu, Okomfo Anokye, and Opoku Ware I, chiefs would not sit down to see their king to be taken away without firing a shot. No European could have dared speak to chiefs of Asanta in the way the governor spoke to you this morning. Is it true that the bravery of Asanta is no more? I cannot believe it. It cannot be! I must say this: if you, the men of Asante, will not go forward, then we will. We, the women, will. I shall call upon my fellow women. We will fight! We will fight till the last of us falls in the battlefields.

He founded the capital town of Kumasi, and designated a golden stool as his throne, a symbol of his power. He established a national army and expanded his empire, which he ruled well. Osei Tutu astutely provided important jobs in his kingdom to the tribal leaders whom he had conquered. Other chiefs under his rule agreed to pay taxes for the purchase of guns and to travel to the capital whenever they were summoned.

In 1698, the Ashanti began a war with a neighboring kingdom, Denkyera. That kingdom stood between the Ashanti and the coast and controlled all trade of the Ashanti. After three years, the Denkyera were defeated. In the reign of the next Ashanti king, Opuku Ware, more tribes in the interior were conquered, until by 1750 most of the tribes of the interior formed parts of

When Europeans first began to trade with the people of Ghana, their chief interests were gold and ivory, but another commodity quickly became even more profitable.

By the early 1700s, slavery was the most important trade between the Europeans and the Africans. Ashanti raiding parties armed with European weapons bought from traders penetrated the interior and captured innocent people, whom they then herded to the coastal forts to sell. The forts became prisons, holding pens, and slave markets. Countless hundreds of people were imprisoned in the filthy, insanitary holds of trading ships for the journey to the Americas. Many died from disease or starvation, or were murdered by the ships' captains.

The vigorous slave trade continued for another hundred years. The Ashanti became the richest and most powerful empire in West Africa through the combination of military might, the sale of enemies, and the profits made from both activities. The trade was finally stopped early in the nineteenth century, when first Denmark, then Britain, and finally America outlawed the slave trade and sent ships to capture the slave ships and return them with their human cargoes to Africa.

the Ashanti Empire. The last kingdom to hold out against the onrush of the Ashanti was the Fanti Empire, which dominated the coastal area, and with it the prized trade with Europeans. In 1750, however, Opuku Ware died and civil war broke out among his potential successors. Several subject kingdoms seized the opportunity to declare their independence and join the Fanti Empire. After that, the Ashanti Empire began to decline, weakened by wars and a string of bad kings.

Osei Bonsu became leader of the Ashanti in 1801. Under his rule, the strength of the Ashanti grew once more. His armies finally defeated the Fanti in 1807, and the Ashanti became the most powerful empire in West Africa, controlling most of modern Ghana.

BRITISH TRADE AND CONTROL

This engraving depicts British travelers sailing on the Volta in the nineteenth century.

As the Europeans became more established on the coast of Ghana, the British saw the growing power of the Ashanti as a threat to their own power. The British had developed trading relations with the Fanti tribe. Rising Ashanti power threatened British military power, while the British alliance posed a challenge to Ashanti power. The Ashanti began attacking British forts, while the British continued to provide military support to the Fanti.

When the slave trade was finally abolished in Europe in the early nineteenth century, the British hoped that by destroying the Ashanti they could end the slave trade in Africa. In 1821, a British governor, Sir Charles MacCarthy, was installed to administer the area, but he was killed by the Ashanti in 1824. The British eventually defeated the Ashanti in 1826. In 1829, George Maclean, a British military officer, was sent to Ghana to sign a peace treaty with the Ashanti. The British agreed to protect Ashanti traders and to arbitrate in intertribal disputes. On their part, the Ashanti and other tribes consented to stop human sacrifices and to keep the peace. In that new peace, trade again began to flourish. Palm oil, pepper, and corn were added to gold and ivory as valuable exports, while imports included tools, alcohol, tobacco, and guns.

In 1844, the British sent out a new governor to work with Maclean. The governor and his successors started raising taxes among the local ethnic groups to finance road building. That was very unpopular and led to attacks on British trading posts. In 1867, the British and Dutch agreed to divide the Ghanaian coast between them, with the British taking the east and the Dutch the west.

In 1868 the Fanti organized a confederation to oppose the British and to defend themselves against the Ashanti. The British saw this new alliance as a threat to their authority and arrested its leaders, leaving the confederation to fade away. The British began buying all the Dutch forts and by 1874 had become the sole European power in Ghana.

The main remaining native African threat was the Ashanti, who lost their allies and source of guns when the Dutch left. The British attacked the Ashanti in 1874, burning their capital, Kumasi. Afterward, they initially allowed the Ashanti their independence, but in 1891, fearing that the French might annex the Ashanti territories, they declared the Ashanti kingdom a protectorate. The Ashanti challenged the declaration. In 1896, the British attacked Kumasi for the second time, exiling the ruler to Sierra Leone. During the 1890s, the British extended their power to the north of Ghana. By 1902, newly drawn borders formed the British colony named the Gold Coast.

This nineteenth-century engraving shows the traditional dress of the Ashanti.

THE TWENTIETH CENTURY

Ghana had only reluctantly become a colony in the British Empire. In the past, the British had exerted just enough control to keep the exports flowing, but once Ghana was a colony, the priorities changed. A governor was appointed, with two councils (the legislative and executive councils) to help him make decisions. All the people who sat on these councils were British until 1914, when nine of the legislative councilors were Ghanaians. In 1943, two Africans joined the executive council. The legislative council functioned as a ratifying body for the laws that the governor introduced. By using a system of indirect rule, where the local chiefs acted as executives of the governor's laws, the British bypassed the intellectual elite of Ghana who might have challenged British authority if they were given any power.

In some ways, the British brought peace and advancement to Ghana. The first gold mines were developed, where previously gold dust had been

The Independence Arch stands in Independence Square in Accra.

panned from rivers. Manganese, bauxite, and diamond mines were also created. Railways were built to carry the products of the mines to the coast, and harbors were constructed for the ships that came to collect the exports. The government distributed cocoa beans to local farmers and encouraged the cocoa industry. Towns sprang up as a result of trade and the railways, and in the growing towns the government also built hospitals and schools.

For many Ghanaians, however, those gestures were inadequate compensation for the massive profits that British companies were making from the labor of the Ghanaians. Until 1948, there were no universities in Ghana; if an African wanted a university education, he had to go overseas to study. The question of whether "colonization" was anything but foreign predation was and remains real.

INDEPENDENCE

One of the aspiring students who went abroad was Kwame Nkrumah. In the United States, he studied Karl Marx and the writings of African Americans and developed radical ideas about independence for Ghana. In Ghana at that time there was already a pro-independence party that campaigned for a gradual shift to independence. In 1949, Nkrumah broke away from that party and, with the slogan "Self-Government Now," shaped a more vocal and radical party, the Convention People's Party (CPP).

Jerry Rawlings

In 1951, when Nkrumah was in jail for his party's campaign disturbances, the CPP won the general election. Nkrumah was released and asked to form a government. For six years, Nkrumah and his party compromised, working with the colonial powers and at the same time learning about the workings of government. In 1957, power passed peacefully to the people of Ghana when Great Britain granted the country independence.

Ghana was the first African colony south of the Sahara to gain political power; unfortunately, it went into a tailspin. At independence, Ghana held half a billion US dollars in reserves. Ten years later, it was a billion dollars in debt. Foreign loans were taken out to finance ill-conceived projects such as the Volta (Akosombo) Dam. Income plunged when the international price of cocoa collapsed. Many industries were nationalized and began losing money. From a peak of popularity throughout Africa in 1957, Kwame Nkrumah gradually resorted to one-party rule and ordered numerous arrests of political opponents to cling to power. An attempted coup failed in 1962, but in 1966, while he was abroad, another coup was successfully carried out. Nkrumah never returned to Ghana.

Between 1966 and 1981, a series of corrupt governments ran Ghana. For three years, the government was run by a National Liberation Council and right-wing elements that hunted down left-wing politicians and parties. Nationalized industries were reprivatized. In 1969, elections were held, and a politically moderate party took power. But the economy was so weak that food shortages and crushing price increases developed. In 1972, another takeover threw out that government. Military juntas seized power, food prices stayed high, corruption again became widespread, and political opponents were arrested.

In June 1979, yet another overthrow, led by Flight Lieutenant Jerry Rawlings, succeeded. That takeover was, however, different from the earlier coups. Rawlings had made the eradication of corruption his main promise—and he kept his word. Many corrupt officials were arrested and executed. Within a few months, Rawlings had given up power and established a new democratically elected government. But that government fared little better than previous ones. A new set of corrupt politicians began siphoning off much-needed state income.

In 1981, Rawlings led his second coup, promising once more to remove corrupt practices and restore stability to the economy. This time, Rawlings decided to keep the power and sort out the problems himself. Rawlings's ideas were very left wing. There were several attempts by other factions of the army to depose him, but all failed. Jerry Rawlings remained popular with Ghanaians at the grassroots level, and he oversaw a gradual improvement in the economy. Rawlings was elected president in 1992, in the first election held since 1979. In 1996, he held general elections and was reelected to office, a people's president in a stable country. John Agyekum Kufuor was the next president, from 2001 until January 2009, when John Evans Atta Mills assumed that office.

RECENT EVENTS

In 2012, Ghana suffered the premature death of President Mills. He died in office, a few months before Ghana's next presidential election, in which Mills was running for a second term. He was replaced by his vice president, John Dramani Mahama, who went on to narrowly win the election.

In the same year, Ghana suffered two major displacements of civilians. Violent uprisings occurred in Hohoe municipality, in the north of the nation, when mounting disagreement over the burial of Muslims led to the outright ban of Muslim burial rites in particular neighborhoods. A local imam died, was buried in defiance of the ban, and the body was exhumed and left by the road. Local Muslims rose up in violent protest, and the disruption was enough to prompt many Ghanaians to flee the region.

The second displacement led to the eventual deportation of illegal Chinese immigrants who had arrived hoping to win access to Ghanaian gold in the southwestern Ashanti Plateau. Over a period of more than a decade, Chinese nationals had smuggled themselves into Ghana and set up illegal gold mines. The government in 2012 chose to repatriate them and close up legal loopholes. They were determined to prevent foreign exploitation of Ghanaian resources and citizens.

In 2016, Nana Addo Dankwa Akufo-Addo led his New Patriotic Party to victory, and Ghana experienced its third peaceful transfer of power between opposing parties since 1992. Ghana is widely considered a stable democracy with high ratings for human rights. There are lingering issues that confront Ghana, including conflicts over the use of resources, exploitation by non-Ghanaian nations and corporations, and concerns over illegal immigration. However, Ghana remains a stable and remarkably peaceful nation. As evidence of this, in 2018, the World Press Freedom Index ranked Ghana number one in Africa for the freedom of its press. Not only is Ghana the top African nation in this regard, but it also outranks the United States.

Nana Addo Dankwa Akufo-Addo was elected president of Ghana in 2016.

INTERNET LINKS

http://www.bbc.com/news/world-africa-13434226
This BBC timeline examines important events in Ghana's history.

https://www.ghanaweb.com/GhanaHomePage/history
GhanaWeb offers information about Ghana's history.

http://www.historyworld.net/wrldhis/PlainTextHistories.asp?historyid=ad43
This History World reference site provides a general history of Ghana.

GOVERNMENT

The Flagstaff House is used as Ghana's presidential palace.

3

ON JANUARY 7, 2017, NANA ADDO Dankwa Akufo-Addo was sworn in as Ghana's fifth president. He had defeated the incumbent John Dramani Mahama by 10 percent of the vote. Nana Konadu Agyemang-Rawlings, the widow of Jerry Rawlings, also ran for president, although she was disqualified during the campaign for alleged improper filing. Jerry Rawlings was a hero of Ghana's government reform movement during the 1970s and 1980s. He planned two successful coups in the process of reforming Ghana and served as the first president elected under the current constitution. His widow carried both the prestige and the baggage of those prior associations. Akufo-Addo, a human rights lawyer, promised a return to stability during a period of economic downturn.

"Ghana will not be built in a day. But it should be built every day and the body that houses the eyes reading this owns the hands that will ensure this."

—Nana Awere Damoah

Nana Addo Dankwa Akufo-Addo

GHANA'S CONSTITUTION

Four constitutions have been adopted since Ghana's independence. The current one dates to 1992. It calls for a multiparty system, with one legislative house of 275 members elected by direct, universal adult suffrage. The executive functions of the government are carried out by the president, a council of ministers approved by the legislature, and a vice president. There is also a National Security Council, made up of senior ministers and members of the security forces. Beside the national government, there is a system of tribal governments led by chiefs.

GHANA'S PRESIDENT

The president is the head of state of Ghana and head of government. In 1992, Jerry Rawlings was the first president to be elected under the current constitution. The president and vice president are elected on the same ticket by popular vote for a term of four years, with a possibility of a second term. In the December 2016 election, there were seven candidates, including the incumbent president, John Dramani Mahama; Nana Konadu Agyemang-Rawlings; and the ultimate victor, Nana Addo Dankwa Akufo-Addo. The swearing-in marked the third peaceful transfer of power between parties in this previously unstable nation. Akufo-Addo received a strong majority of about 54 percent, compared with Mahama's 44 percent, giving him a stable and positive start to his term of office. The next closest contender gained only 1 percent, suggesting Akufo-Addo can rely on a strong following for some time to come.

POLITICAL PARTIES

During the first decade of Rawlings's administration, political parties were banned in Ghana. They were legalized for the 1992 election, although none of Ghana's previous parties were allowed to register for the election. Today, Ghana has a multiparty system, although two main political parties—the

JERRY RAWLINGS

Jerry John Rawlings was born in 1947, to a Ghanaian mother and Scottish father. He was educated in Ghana, first at Achimoto College and then at the military college. In 1969, he was commissioned a lieutenant in the air force. Ten years later, he led a military coup against the corrupt civilian government of Ignatius Kutu Acheampong. Acheampong and many others were tried and executed. Rawlings kept power for 112 days and then called a general election. Two years later, after the failure of the next president to prevent corruption or improve the economy, Rawlings led a second coup and this time held on to power, ruling with the aid of the Provisional National Defense Council.

Local committees were set up to monitor the work of factories and run local neighborhoods. In 1983, Rawlings switched from his Marxist policies to free-market ones, denationalizing state-owned industries, devaluing the currency, and abandoning price controls. All these measures were very unpopular, but people realized that he had Ghana's interests at heart and accepted them. Ghana become one of the few African countries with a healthy economy and relatively stable government under his presidency.

New Patriotic Party (NPP) and National Democratic Congress (NDC)—typically hold power, and it is difficult for other parties to gain representation in government. The National Democratic Congress held power under former president John Dramani Mahama, while the New Patriotic Party has held power since 2017 with President Akufo-Addo. Smaller parties include the Convention People's Party (CPP) and the People's National Convention (PNC).

THE COURTS

The judicial system is based on English legal practice. In addition to statutory laws, there are customary laws and the English structure of common law, which

The Supreme Court of Ghana

is a series of laws not written down but accepted by the legal system. The superior courts are the Supreme Court, the Court of Appeal, the High Court, and regional tribunals; the lesser courts are the circuit courts, district courts, and juvenile courts. Dissolved for a time during military rule, the Supreme Court has been reestablished as the court of final appeal. Its chief justice and eleven other justices exercise jurisdiction over the interpretation and enforcement of constitutional law. Outside of this system, the Commission on Human Rights and Administrative Justice investigates corruption and abuse of public office.

TRIBAL RULE

The traditional system of government in Ghana has outlasted numerous military and civilian governments, as well as British rule. In ancient times, each

One unusual tribal chief of Ghana is Lynne Symonds, a schoolteacher born and bred in Sunderland, England. In 1996, she became the first female tribal chief in Ghana when she was made a chief of the Mamprugipuiginaba clan in honor of her organizing aid to the poverty-stricken villages of northern Ghana. She is currently an honorary chief of

three different tribes, was granted a "Points of Light" award by British prime minister David Cameron in 2015, and continues to be an active force in both the Ghanaian House of Chiefs and in charitable efforts in her nation.

ethnic group had its own ruler who dominated life in his tribal area—often as small as a few villages but sometimes extending across the country. The chief traditionally ruled with the help of a council of elders and could call on the loyalty of the villages that he administered in times of war. Below that ruler was a series of local and village chiefs who sat on his council of elders and could depose a bad chief at will. The British used the tribal chieftaincies to wield control during colonial times, and the system remains in place today.

A tribal court is presided over by the tribe's chief.

Before the British came, the clan chief had power over all aspects of life and law. The British accepted the chiefs' rule over tribal matters but sat as a court of appeal when clan disputes threatened to escalate to war. Since independence in 1957, the successive national governments have retained this classic tribal system in Ghana, while gradually reducing its power.

After 1957, Regional Houses of Chiefs were set up that elected representatives to sit in a national House of Chiefs. A ministry was set up to oversee tribal matters such as land rights and the appointment, removal, and succession of new chiefs. A separate judicial system has even been used to adjudicate in disputes between individuals and their chiefs.

THE ARMED FORCES

Since 1957, the army has played a leading role in the government of Ghana. For twenty-five years, the army was responsible for many coups: all were relatively popular and targeted at corrupt civil governments. The armed forces of 13,500 troops, composed of both men and women, is comparatively small. The nation currently has a defense budget of $120 million, and the service is ranked 101 out of 133 nations.

Soldiers in the Ghanaian military march during drills.

FOREIGN POLICY

Ghana's recent foreign policy has emphasized good relations with its close neighbors. There is careful coordination of currencies, trade, infrastructure, and education with neighbors within the Economic Community of West African States (ECOWAS). The rest of Africa and other countries also enjoy friendly relations with Ghana. Ghana practices economic diplomacy that facilitates trade, tourism, and investments in such key sectors as energy, agriculture and agro-processing, information and communication technology (ICT), infrastructural development (ports and roadways), and the tourist industry. Beginning in 2017, President Donald Trump's restrictive stance on immigration created some stress between Ghana and the United States.

GHANA'S FIRST PRIME MINISTER

Kwame Nkrumah, Ghana's first prime minister and, later, president, was a powerful and popular leader. He was born in 1909, in what was then the British Gold Coast colony. After teaching in the colony for some years, Nkrumah left for Lincoln University in the United States to study politics, particularly the theories of Marx, Lenin, and Marcus Garvey, the 1920s black Jamaican leader who worked for years in the United States in the cause of all blacks. Nkrumah returned to the Gold Coast in 1947, at the invitation of the United Gold Coast Convention (UGCC), a party agitating for independence.

Nkrumah became very popular, speaking at meetings all over the country. In 1948, after several riots, he was arrested, along with other UGCC leaders, on suspicion of organizing the riots, but he was soon released. The next year, he split with the UGCC, which he considered too middle class, and founded a new party based on a principle of immediate self-government, the Convention People's Party (CPP). In 1950, he orchestrated a series of demonstrations, strikes, and noncooperation activities. In the ensuing civil disruption, Nkrumah was arrested for the second time and sentenced to a year's imprisonment.

In 1951, while still in jail, Nkrumah was elected to parliament in a massive demonstration of political support. In 1952, the people's champion became

Born on March 29, 1944, President Nana Addo Dankwa Akufo-Addo is native to Ga-Maami, in the Nima area of Ghana's capital city, Accra. He was educated at the Government Boy's School and the Rowe Road School in Ghana, then went to the United Kingdom (UK) to study at Lansing College, in Sussex, before taking his O- and A-level tests qualifying him

A statue of Akufo-Addo (*left*) stands in Owerri, Nigeria, alongside statues of other African leaders.

for advanced education. He began a course of study at New College, Oxford, in 1962, but chose to return to Ghana after a short time. Back in his home nation, he enrolled at the Accra Secondary School, then entered the University of Ghana at Legon, where he studied economics, graduating with a bachelor's degree in economics in 1967.

Akufo-Addo returned to the UK, where he studied law. He was called to the English Bar (Middle Temple) in 1971, followed by the Ghanaian Bar in 1975. He had a career in human rights law and was based at various times in both France and Ghana.

Before his election to the office of president in 2016, Akufo-Addo served his nation in multiple roles. He was the general secretary for the People's Movement for Freedom and Justice and the first national organizer of the New Patriotic Party. He was elected to Ghana's legislature and also served in Ghana's cabinet—as attorney general and minister for justice, and later as foreign minister.

After losing in the 2008 and 2012 presidential elections, Akufo-Addo was finally elected on the New Patriotic Party ticket in 2016, and he was sworn in as president on January 7, 2017. He is the husband of Rebecca Akufo-Addo. They are parents to five daughters and have five grandchildren.

prime minister of the Gold Coast. He served as prime minister for five years under British rule and oversaw the peaceful transition to independence. His style of government then changed abruptly, and he began imprisoning people without trial. Nevertheless, his public building programs kept him popular with ordinary countrymen. In 1960, he became president of the Republic of Ghana under Ghana's second constitution.

Always interested in black African politics, President Nkrumah began to champion the idea of African unity—a single African state of massive size and power. His development projects grew more and more expensive and unrealistic, and soon Ghana was in debt to foreign powers. As dissent grew, Nkrumah began to exert his political control in an increasingly draconian way. An attempt was made on his life in 1962, and he withdrew from public view. Ghana became a one-party state, and food shortages made life hard for Ghanaians everywhere. While on a visit to Beijing in 1966, Nkrumah was deposed by the police and army. He died in exile in 1972 in Romania, while receiving treatment for throat cancer.

INTERNET LINKS

http://www.ghana.gov.gh
This is the official government of Ghana website.

https://www.modernghana.com
Modern Ghana is an online newspaper that often covers political happenings in the country.

ECONOMY

The spillway and power station at Lake Volta Dam

4

MODERN GHANA IS AMONG THE most economically prosperous and stable of the African nations, with an economy that has recovered from early abuses and which is weathering current global change. The double disaster of early economic overreach in the form of grandiose programs and of administrative corruption and mismanagement led to rocky times in Ghana's early independence. The Volta Dam, which has provided some long-term benefits, also overextended Ghana's available funds and unbalanced the economy. It took time to develop a stable, deep culture of money management among civilian, military, and government administrators, but now Ghana's long-term economic prospects are strong.

The stability of the Jerry Rawlings years and tough economic policies helped reverse Ghana's decline and sparked renewed foreign interest in investing in the country's renewal. His government worked to arrest inflation, reschedule overseas debt repayment, increase agricultural productivity, and encourage exportation of locally manufactured goods. Conditions were looking much better by the 1990s.

Ghana has always been rich in natural resources, especially gold. Industries based on those resources came back in production. The Rawlings administration sought the help of the International Monetary Fund (IMF), which recommended an economic recovery program aimed at a free-market economy, tight control of spending, and the removal of subsidies for staple foods. Although unpopular, those straightforward measures won acceptance.

Ghana's economy, a mixture of private and public enterprise, is based on agriculture and mining, and its chief exports are gold and cocoa. Accra has become the main artery through which Ghana's exports are moved and luxury commodities enter the country.

Many African countries are producers of primary products, such as minerals and crops, and their well-being depends on world commodity prices that are controlled by markets far away in the international financial centers. Prices

A woman displays freshly dyed kente cloth.

can fall and wipe out a country's income. For instance, in the mid-1960s cocoa prices collapsed, pushing Ghana's economy into serious decline.

During the years following 2010, Ghana's economy again started to show signs of trouble. By 2016, the economy was weaker than it had been in two decades. Working with the World Bank, President Nana Addo Dankwa Akufo-Addo imposed restrictions and reduced government expenditure. The nation worked with Côte d'Ivoire to settle issues regarding the possession of oil fields. The government is also looking for ways to approach threats to the cocoa crop. These things, among others, have brought about a turn-around in the economy, leading to growth for over five quarters as of the end of 2017.

AGRICULTURE

Forty-four percent of Ghana's workforce is employed in agricultural jobs, and over 18 percent of the nation's economy is based in agriculture.

Besides cocoa, Ghana also produces rice, cassava (tapioca), peanuts, corn, shea nuts, bananas, and timber. Bananas were first exported from Ghana in 1929. They are grown in the southeast, in the forested region, where the weather is warm and humid. Banana production is difficult because the fruit is delicate and easily damaged. It has to be picked when unripe and kept in special cool containers. Fortunately, in Ghana the growing areas are near the southern seaports, so the bananas can be transported quickly and are less likely to be damaged.

Cola nuts, the basic ingredient of the many cola drinks consumed around the world, are a lucrative industry in Ghana. Cola trees need the same environment as cocoa, so the two crops may compete for the same available space on farms. Cola trees, however, grow faster and so are used as shade trees for young cacao plants—the two plants are often seen growing together.

Coconuts are grown along the coast. They were first grown commercially after 1920, when the British colonial government set up plantations and nurseries and distributed seedlings to local farmers to encourage the crop. The main product of coconut trees is copra, the dried meat of their fruit, from which coconut oil is processed. Tobacco is one of the smallest cash crops in Ghana. It has been grown commercially since the 1930s, cultivated in small

The Ministry of Food and Agriculture of the Republic of Ghana recently completed a program focusing on promoting permaculture crops in Ghana, including rubber and oil palms. They hoped that in doing so they would improve the links between small farmers, ensuring better and more efficient use of resources and the development of lasting infrastructure in Ghana's extensive rural regions. Just as permaculture pushes farmers and their communities to invest in long-term planning, it forces the nation itself to invest with the future in mind. The ministry made its own investment through the building of roads in rural areas, consultancies to support associations between farms, and the promotion of effective long-term permanent plantings of crop species.

pockets in various parts of the country. A tobacco company was established in Ghana in 1951.

Sugarcane is grown mostly on a small-scale basis by individual farmers; there are few commercial sugarcane plantations in Ghana. The plant needs plenty of rainfall to thrive and therefore is grown in valleys or in the forested region. Cultivated mostly for domestic consumption, it is also used by the alcohol industry. Factories sited near plantations convert the crop to sugar.

Besides those commercial products, many other crops are grown and either consumed within the villages or sold at local markets. They include corn, millet, groundnuts (peanuts), tomatoes, green vegetables, peppers, cocoyam (a root vegetable), cassava, yams, and plantains.

FISHING AND LIVESTOCK

Fishing is a small domestic industry. Families living along the coast go out in canoes to catch fish to supplement their diet. Larger commercial boats are

COCOA

Cocoa is Ghana's most important cash crop and was once its highest export earner, accounting for some two-thirds of the country's revenue. Recent drops in world cocoa prices reduced Ghana's revenue from this product significantly, though developments as of 2018 suggest this trend has begun to reverse, with revenue from cocoa sales once again on the rise. The crop provides employment to more than half a million people. Cocoa has also historically provided much of the capital for Ghana's many infrastructure projects.

Cocoa was first exported in 1885. In 1890, the colonial government set up a botanical garden to raise cacao seedlings to distribute to local farmers. It is cultivated mostly in forested regions because it needs deep, well-drained soil and a high rainfall throughout the year, although too much rain at any one time can induce disease in the plant.

The cacao crop is first cultivated on forestland that has been cleared of all but the few trees kept to shade the young plants. Additional shade comes from cocoyams and plantains, which also help provide some income while the cacao trees are still small. The trees become productive after about five years. At that stage, the enterprise becomes labor-intensive. Harvesting, which can take three or four months, begins in September. The large, ripe cocoa pods are collected and the beans scooped out and fermented for several days. They are then sun-dried for about two weeks and packed into bags for shipment to processors.

motorized and use nets to catch tuna, bream, and herring. A state fishing agency operates a fleet of trawlers, and there are some private foreign-owned fishing fleets. In the north of the country, there are a few small fish farms. Lake Volta provides a useful supply of freshwater fish. The many lagoons along the coast are another source of seafood. Tema, 16 miles (26 km) from Accra, is Ghana's largest fishing port.

Cattle are raised commercially on a small scale in the coastal savanna areas such as the Accra Plains. The total head of cattle produced, however, falls far short of demand, and most of the beef consumed in Ghana is imported. The drier northern region is ideal for raising cattle, but there cattle traditionally represent wealth. Therefore, many thousands of cattle are herded but usually not for meat, being too valuable to eat. Raising cattle is difficult in many areas because of seasonal water shortages, and because no feed crop is grown.

MANUFACTURING

Countries that have developed manufacturing industries have far more stable economies than countries that depend on primary production such as agriculture. World prices of manufactured goods are more unchanging than those of staples. Establishing a manufacturing base, though, is expensive and risky, with high outlays in infrastructure, research and development, workforce training, and the much more complex administration needed for manufactured goods.

When Ghana was a colony, all primary products were exported to Britain and processed there. After independence, both local entrepreneurs and the various governments realized the importance of developing a manufacturing base. Nonetheless, by 1960 only 8.6 percent of the working population was engaged in manufacturing.

The Rawlings government created a climate conducive to investment; as a result, manufacturing grew by about 9 percent a year. By the 1990s, manufacturing amounted to 14 percent of the GDP (gross domestic product). The sector then declined steadily from a GDP of 9 percent in 2000 to 8.1 percent in 2007, reflecting the worldwide energy crisis. After a slight increase, manufacturing declined to 5.6 percent in 2018. Ghana's food-processing industries include sugar refineries, flour mills, and several cocoa-processing factories where Ghanaian chocolate is made. The country also has beef-processing plants, dairy products works, vegetable-oil mills that produce coconut and palm oil, and small tomato and pineapple factories. There are several breweries making beer from imported hops, a soft-drink industry, and cigarette factories.

Cotton is grown in Ghana as well as imported. Cotton fibers are woven into cloth and then into clothing in factories ringed around the southern cities. Jute, kenaf, and roselle are other fiber plants grown in Ghana that are turned into cloth, rope, and sacks in small factories.

Women work with textiles in a Ghanaian factory.

The forestry industry supports sawmills, furniture and boat building, and the manufacture of plywood and paper products. Ghana also has oil refineries that process kerosene, gasoline, and diesel fuel; cement works and brick factories using imported materials; and chemical plants that make medicines, insecticides, and paints.

ELECTRICITY

Before 1966, when the Volta hydroelectric plant at the foot of Lake Volta was opened, electricity was produced by small diesel generators. The new power plant supplied electricity to Accra and the towns of southern Ghana. Most of its newfound electric power went to the aluminum smelting plant nearby, but for several years the power supply was inadequate because of operating problems and a series of droughts. Since 1981, the system has been improved and extended. Now almost all the major towns receive electricity, and Ghana even sells electricity to neighboring countries.

Ghana has traditionally used hydroelectric resources to generate electricity because hydroelectric is among the least expensive power sources. In a nation with regular droughts, however, energy production has proven erratic. Recently, Ghana has started looking for ways to diversify its sources of energy in order to provide more reliable electricity for more of the nation.

FORESTRY AND MINING

Gold, diamonds, manganese, and bauxite are mined in Ghana. Gold mining slumped after independence, but the beautiful metal has recently begun to catch up with cocoa as a leading export. Ghana's diamonds are mostly of

A rope bridge extends over Kakum National Park in southern Ghana.

industrial grade rather than jewelry grade. The nation is also the world's eighth-largest producer of manganese, with mines in the western region. There are large reserves of bauxite in Ghana, but the mining of it is not developed, and most of the raw bauxite used in aluminum manufacturing is imported. In recent years, foreign companies have shown an increasing interest in Ghana's mineral resources. Over the past decade, oil production has become a reliable fraction of Ghana's income, as the nation and its neighbors begin to capitalize on regional offshore oil.

Ghana's forest reserves have been exploited for decades, particularly during the 1960s. After a decline in production in the 1970s and 1980s, the country's timber resources are now being managed better, and exports are on the rise. Ghana has projected sufficient reserves until the year 2030. Preservation efforts are still in the early stages, however, with little done to compensate for the loss of forest reserves through both logging and areas cleared for cocoa production.

TRANSPORTATION

Ghana's chief means of transportation are roads, railways, rivers, Lake Volta, and air. In the more rural and undeveloped north of the country, horses and donkeys are still used. Transportation routes are linked in the major areas of economic production, connecting them with urban centers and ultimately with Accra. Roads for cars and trucks were first constructed in the early years of the twentieth century, linking the southern towns, and then they were extended to the cacao plantations in the southwest.

Like much of Ghana's economy, the road system was not kept up during the 1970s and 1980s, but since then many roads have been paved and cared for. Asphalt roads string along the coast, joining the coastal towns, and lead to Kumasi in the center of Ghana and then northward to Tamale. Similar roads link the other major towns. A freeway that runs from Accra to Tema was expanded from two to three lanes between 2014 and 2016. Other roads are smaller and unsurfaced and are often swept away altogether in the rainy season, making travel difficult.

While effort has been made to maintain and improve Ghanaian roads in the past decade, increasing urban populations, improving trade levels, and overall economic growth have increased road use and put enormous pressure on Ghana's still developing transportation infrastructure.

Railways extend across the country, linking major production areas with Accra. The railways are largely used to move freight. Schedules are irregular, so trains are unpopular as public transportation. Many of Ghana's rivers are not navigable, but the dam at Akosombo has created the huge Lake Volta that makes water transportation from the north cheap and convenient. Ports have been built around the lake to facilitate this increasingly popular mode of travel. Ghana has small airports at Sekondi-Takoradi, Kumasi, Sunyani, and Tamale, in addition to the Kotoka International Airport in Accra.

Since 2013, Ghana has sought foreign investors to help expand its rail services, focusing in particular on the Eastern Corridor, which connects the nation's largest port in Tema with the capital city, other urban areas, and Burkina Faso.

Railroads extend throughout the major cities in Ghana.

INTERNET LINKS

http://countrystudies.us/ghana/63.htm
This website offers historical context for Ghana's economy.

https://www.heritage.org/index/country/Ghana
The Heritage Organization provides analysis on Ghana's economic freedom.

https://www.nytimes.com/2018/03/10/world/africa/ghana-worlds -fastest-growing-economy.html
This *New York Times* article explores Ghana's booming economy.

ENVIRONMENT

The effects of debris and pollution are a major concern in Ghana.

5

AT THE START OF INDEPENDENCE, Ghana faced many long-term challenges in terms of modernization. Hoping to become a fully industrial nation, the country required stable power sources. With only one major river, the Volta, no significant coal or oil known at that time, and no great hope of nuclear power, there seemed little choice but to dam the one major river system they did have. Thus, the Volta Dam was an obvious and probably unavoidable project. However, Ghana's leadership was not prepared for the challenges that would follow. The newly created water reservoirs spread waterborne diseases. Regional communities were destroyed or displaced, and wildlife ecologies were eradicated. All in all, the Volta Dam created many problems, while failing to fully resolve those for which it was proposed.

"To live is to choose. But to choose well, you must know who you are and what you stand for, where you want to go and why you want to get there."
—Kofi Annan, Ghanaian diplomat and former secretary-general of the United Nations

Joshua Amponsem is a powerful young environmental activist. He holds a degree in environmental science and has served as a vocal advocate in the Ghanaian movement to protect the environment. His work is widely recognized by a diverse range of institutions. The Massachusetts Institute of Technology (MIT) has declared him the first "World Climate Ambassador" for West Africa. The Global Peace Initiative of Women has named him a fellow. Amponsem founded the Green Africa Youth Organization, a nonprofit organization that advocates for environmental sustainability, and serves as research and outreach coordinator for Ghana Youth Climate Coalition.

POLLUTION

"The gas goes to your nose and you feel something in your head. Then you get sick in your head and chest," says a young man who, with his friends and family, makes a living selling reusable parts of electronics. The leftover scrap plastic is then burned at the dump.

As recently as 2009, the US Environmental Protection Agency (EPA) estimated that thirty to forty million personal computers a year were ready for "end-of-life management" when memory and graphic demands escalate beyond the capacity of the computer. Other consumer electronics such as televisions and cell phones exacerbate the massive problem. That has resulted in a new, deadly kind of waste—electronic waste. It is almost impossible to gauge how much electronic waste is dumped in West African countries such as Ghana, Nigeria, and Côte d'Ivoire from Europe and other countries.

Along the sidewalks of Agbogbloshie Market in Accra, battered Pentium 2 and 3 computers, broken monitors, old television sets that receive only analog signals, cell phones, and other digital hardware and equipment are piled 10 feet (3 m) high. A report published in the *Annals of Global Health* in 2016 estimated there were between 31 and 115 contaminated sites per million inhabitants in Ghana, the result of the toxic waste trade.

Working items are put up for sale; loads of old broken ones are sold for a pittance to scrap dealers, who make their living stripping off resalable components such as drives, memory chips, copper, and other metals to make a dollar or two from a scrap-metal buyer. What cannot be exchanged for money is burned. Tires are used for fuel to burn the valueless relics, releasing carcinogens and other toxic particles into the air. While the adults collect and

This dump in Accra is overflowing.

count their gains, children tend to the burning piles, sending great pillars of lethal black smoke billowing up. The scrap dealers, most of them either related or friends, scurry through the acrid haze feeling sick in the head and chest, compromising health and safety when speed is the key to making money. Discarded parts that cannot turn to ash are thrown into the lagoon to be flushed out to the Gulf of Guinea by the rain.

The shipping and dumping of toxic waste in the country exposes Ghanaian children to high levels of lead, phthalates, and chlorinated dioxins that are known to promote cancer and to cause other impediments to natural health. The exposure is not secondary or passive, but results in many cases from child labor practices that place children on the front lines, dealing with pollutants without protection. Environmental experts in Ghana are educating the public and urging the electronics industry to phase out toxic chemicals in the making of their products or to set up recycling programs to safely dispose of the remains.

Construction of a dam on the Volta River began in the early l960s, and the dam was in operation by 1966. The lake that was created behind it stretches 250 miles (400 km). The long, thin Lake Volta flooded 2.1 million acres (850,000 hectares) of inhabited land (3.6 percent of Ghana's total landmass), and eighty thousand people had to be resettled. The hydroelectric power generated by the Volta Dam supplies a power grid covering southern Ghana and extending into Togo.

The lake provides an inland waterway system that reduces the cost of transporting goods from the north to the south of the country. Its waters irrigate parts of the Accra Plains, which had no steady source of water. It is also likely, in the long run, to affect the country's climate by making the area more humid and increasing rainfall.

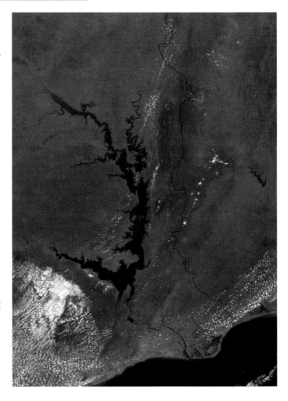

AFTERMATH OF DAM PROJECTS

Regular droughts over the past three decades have resulted in an erratic power supply, which also severely affected agricultural activities in Ghana. The giant Volta River Project, encompassing the Volta and Kpong dams built in the 1960s and 1970s, provided the much-needed electricity to sustain Ghana's domestic and industrial power needs in the early independent years. The impoundment of the Volta River at the two sites, however, has also caused a reduction in the flow of the river, both upstream and downstream. That slowdown has resulted in an invasion of aquatic weeds that today squeeze navigable space, causing silting and closure of the estuary where the Volta meets the Gulf of Guinea.

Most of Ghana's power supply comes from its dams. Another large dam, completed in 2013, was built at Bui on the Black Volta River to minimize Ghana's dependence on imported fuel. The Bui Dam project submerged a quarter of the 700 square miles (1,800 sq km) of Bui National Park, home to more than a hundred rare black hippopotamuses and species of monkeys, lions, buffalo, monitor lizards, antelope, and leopards. Thousands of humans were also forced to relocate, with resultant costs. The altered flow of the Black Volta also negatively impacts the habitats of forty-six species of fish that are economically important to local Ghanaians. Prolonged drought from climate change could severely constrain the dam's capacity. The government has promised to work alongside a variety of agencies to mitigate the negative environmental, social, and ecological impact of dam projects.

The energy crisis and recurrent droughts in Ghana severely affected its economy and agricultural activities. Ghanaians saw the colossal hydropower project on the Volta River as the answer. In addition to generating electric

"While (Ghana's) policies reflect climate action, implementation has not reflected much effort. Sustainable production and consumption is neither implemented nor communicated adequately. Water bodies are being destroyed and water, sanitation, and hygiene infrastructure is poor." —Joshua Amponsem

Droughts have been devastating to farmers in northern Ghana.

Like many other countries where the population is growing, the land in Ghana is coming under increasing pressure as villages expand and the soil becomes depleted. Improved irrigation in the Voltaian Basin encouraged people to raise cattle, and because of this profitable work, large areas of the savanna are being denuded due to overgrazing.

Forested areas are being logged and turned over to grassland and cocoa production. The grassland in turn becomes infertile and overgrazed, and the cocoa plantations disrupt the natural balance of native forests. The result is erosion, as torrential rains fall on what once was vegetation but is now barren soil. Much of the rain forest that has been logged has not been replanted. The government has designated protected reserves where trees cannot be logged and where animals are safe from hunters. Similar solutions will have to be found for the grasslands and cultivated land around the major cities, where the soil is not left fallow (idle) long enough for vegetation to reestablish itself.

power for industry and household energy needs, it was meant to provide large-scale irrigation and modernization of agriculture, and even promote tourism.

Construction of the dams may have solved some problems, but at the same time it created big new ones, such as flooding, waterborne diseases, and the lamentable sacrifice of wildlife habitats. Modernization comes with a price tag to the environment. As of 2018, Ghana is working to diversify its sources of electrical power, providing a more reliable and stable base for the future.

DEFORESTATION

Hardwood forests covered half of Ghana in the late nineteenth century. Today, farming activities and timber exploitation have reduced a dense forest zone of about 30,000 square miles (78,000 sq km) to less than 8,000 square miles (21,000 sq km). That is the result of clearing large tracts of forest for cacao plantations, which thrive in the deep, rich soil of the forest. During times of depressed cocoa prices, timber is sold abroad to generate needed revenue.

Although Ghana bans the export of raw logs and about 5 percent of the land is officially protected, illegal logging threatens the country's remaining forests.

Deforestation also depletes wildlife populations by habitat loss. Since 1988, Ghana has put in place conservation plans and ratified international agreements protecting its forests and endangered species, biodiversity, and the ozone layer.

INTERNET LINKS

http://www.dw.com/en/ecology-versus-economy-in -ghana/a-39853669
This German newspaper provides an analysis of ecological versus economic policies in Ghana, in English.

https://www.researchgate.net/figure/Ecological-zones-of-Ghana_ fig1_221925420
This article explains the ecological zones of Ghana.

https://sciencing.com/ecosystems-ghana-13438.html
This website offers information about the ecosystems of Ghana.

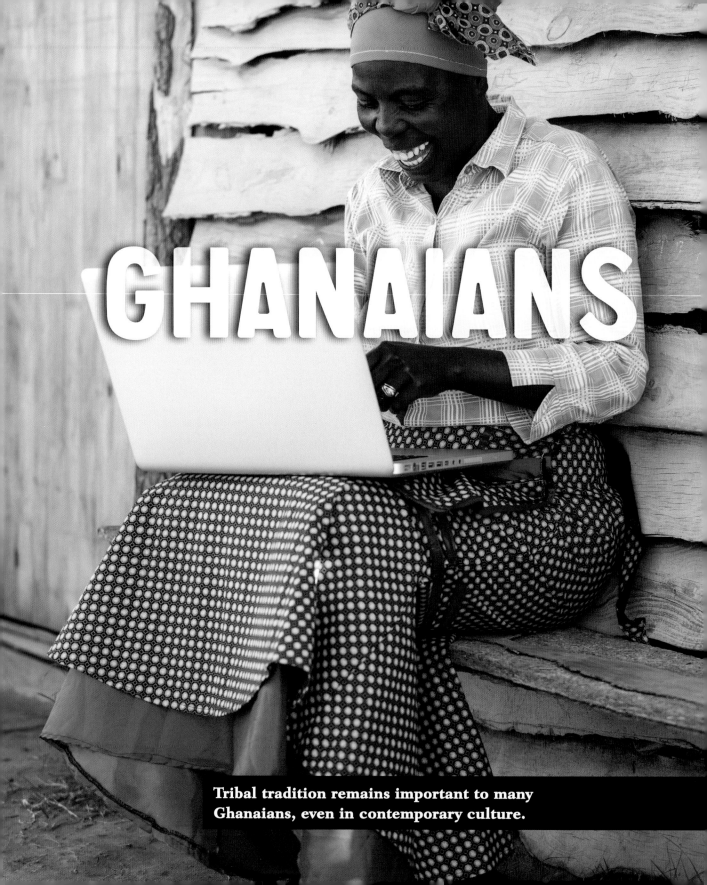

GHANAIANS

Tribal tradition remains important to many Ghanaians, even in contemporary culture.

6

GHANA IS A COUNTRY RICH IN ethnic cultures, with a population of close to twenty-eight million people. Over fifty ethnic groups live in the nation, from the big three tribal families, to smaller tribal representative groups, to immigrants. Each contributes its own traditions, languages, customs, and art. In spite of these differences, Ghana has remained a largely peaceful, welcoming nation, though it does maintain strong control over immigration and foreign activities.

The Akan tribes form the largest ethnic group in Ghana, making up about 48 percent of the population. The Akan are not a single ethnic group, however, and they speak many dialects of their common language.

The northern clans, Dagomba, are more diverse and make up about 17 percent of the population. They have different, unrelated, languages but also speak a common tongue, Dagbani. The Ewe groups live in the Volta region and make up about 14 percent of the population. The Ga and Adangme, who make up 7.5 percent of the population, live mostly in the coastal area around Accra. There are also small populations of a number of other groups.

Another significant division among the peoples of Ghana is that of town and country. About 45 percent of the population lives in the countryside, while 55 percent lives in the cities and suburbs. That division changes continually in favor of city life, as more and more people take commercial jobs instead of agricultural ones. About 74 percent of the population is counted as being economically active, meaning that they take part in the market economy rather than living by subsistence farming. About 45 percent of the working population is in agriculture, while about 41 percent is in service industries such as business, trade, or tourism. The average fertility rate is four children born per woman, which is lower than a number of other African nations.

Ghana does not have the social distinctions based on class or wealth that exist in many European countries. It is essentially an egalitarian society with a tribal structure. Within the tribes, all men are equal, however rich they may be, although in some clans only certain families may become chiefs. But the chiefs are chosen by the people, who can "destool," or unseat, an unpopular chief, removing him from command.

In many of the tribes, property and land are owned by families, not individuals, and are continually redistributed among the family, so few people ever build up personal fortunes or estates. Conversely, few people are really destitute or without family to support them because everyone has a larger group they can count on in times of trouble.

AKAN TRIBES

The Akan tribes, the largest ethnic group in Ghana, live in the southwest and central areas of the country. Subgroups within the Akan group include the Brong, Banda, Adanse, Assin, Twifo, Denkyera, Akyem, Wassa, Akwamu, and Ashanti. The Akan tribes originally lived in the savanna areas in the northwest of Ghana and the northeast of Côte d'Ivoire. They traded cola nuts and gold, which they panned from the rivers, with the people of the coast.

The Akan tribes speak various dialects of the Akan language. Their lives today are often still organized around village communities, with the majority surviving on subsistence farming. Nevertheless, many have migrated to the towns and taken up a modern urban lifestyle.

A subgroup of the Akan are the Fanti (also spelled Fante), who live on the southern coast between Accra and Sekondi-Takoradi. Their oral tradition reports that they moved to the coast from the Ashanti region in the seventeenth century. They grow cassava, cocoyam, and plantains. Many also have small commercial ventures in cocoa, palm oil, and timber.

NORTHERN TRIBAL GROUPS

The Dagomba are one of the major ethnic groups in the north. They are believed to have migrated from east of Lake Chad, across modern Nigeria, and into their present homeland in the north-central region of Ghana. The Dagomba are farmers, growing yam, sorghum, millet, corn, and groundnuts. They also raise cattle and other livestock and live in walled villages. They are among the least affected by modern life.

Akan tribal members attend a funeral.

Because the symbol of a chief's power is the stool he sits on, getting rid of an incompetent, bad, or unpopular chief is called "destooling."

Dagomban children gather in a local village.

The Mamprusi occupy the East and West Mamprusi districts of northern Ghana in the area between the Nasia River and the White Volta. They used to be known in English as Dagomba, but since their southern neighbors appropriated the name, they changed theirs to Mamprusi. They speak several Dagbani languages. Their individual homes are in circular compounds in areas of vegetation known as orchard bush. They are farmers, cultivating crops such as millet, corn, hibiscus, rice, and tobacco. Like the Dagomba, their songs tell of a time when they lived near Lake Chad and migrated to Ghana.

Another ethnic group, the Guan, live in the area where the Black Volta and White Volta Rivers merge. Strangely, in that clan the rulers speak a different language than the ordinary people. The Guan live in small villages of fewer than three hundred people and practice shifting cultivation—that is, farming a piece of land until it is barren and then moving on.

The Fulani are a nomadic band who live throughout West Africa. They speak Fulfulde. Those in Ghana are chiefly herdsmen for hire, looking after the cattle of northern ethnic groups.

The Fanti, once a major power in Ghana and in the British-controlled Gold Coast, have largely migrated to a small portion of the southern coast or immigrated to other West African nations.

OTHER GROUPS

The Ewe live in southeastern Ghana as well as in Benin and the southern half of Togo. Their original home was in modern Benin, but they were driven out by the expansion of the Yoruba Empire in the sixteenth century. They speak a version of the Kwa language and are farmers and fishermen, as well as potters and blacksmiths.

The Ga also live in southeastern Ghana. They are coastal people whose language belongs to part of the Ga-Adangme language system. They arrived in Ghana in the seventeenth century, making their way down the Niger River and across the Volta River. They established the towns of Accra, Osu, Labadi, Teshi, Nunga, and Tema, each new town with a stool as its symbol of leadership and a chief to go with it. Originally farmers, the Ga have branched out into fishing and trade. Unusual among Ghanaians, the main breadwinner in a Ga family is the woman.

Speaking very similar dialects is a group of tribes called the Adangme. They live along the Volta and part of the coast. They are farmers, growing millet, cassava, yams, corn, plantains, and some cash crops.

CLOTHING

In cities of southern Ghana, the typical dress is Western style, with shorts and T-shirts for most men or a suit and tie for businessmen. Women wear dresses or pants cut from imported, patterned cloth or local traditional designs. During elections, funerals, or important political or religious functions, Ghanaians often wear clothes with images of their political leaders to honor them. The traditional cloth of Ghana is called kente cloth. Narrow strips of cloth are woven on small looms and sewn together by hand to make several yards of material. Each pattern woven into the cloth has a story and significance for the various tribes. Women in the cities may have their kente cloth made into dresses, skirts, and blouses.

"The surface of the water is beautiful, but it is no good to sleep on."
—Ghanaian proverb

Take 33 feet (10 m) of cloth and drape it around the back, with the left arm in line with the top edge and the right arm above the top edge.

Gather the cloth in the left hand over the left shoulder.

Take the cloth in the right hand under the right arm and pull it forward over the left shoulder. Both ends of the cloth are now over the left shoulder.

Bring forward the bulk of the cloth, hanging behind the left shoulder, and throw over the left shoulder again. This leaves the right arm and shoulder bare.

A woman selects kente cloth.

Traditional styles of dress vary from region to region. In the north live many Muslims, and their clothing reflects their religious beliefs. Men wear loose-flowing, full-length robes, usually blue, white, or a dark color.

In the south, the cloth is patterned in bright colors. A man's traditional attire is made of 26 to 33 feet (8 to 10 m) of cloth draped in a very specific way and often worn over a shirt and shorts. At funerals, the common color to wear is black. It is also appropriate to wear red at the funerals of relatives. White, which represents joy and victory, can be worn at the death of an octogenarian or older. Women must wear a black cloth wound around the head.

Women's traditional dress consists of three garments and a girdle, or sash. The first is a loose blouse. The second is a large piece of cloth wrapped around the waist, forming a floor-length skirt. The blouse is tucked into the girdle, which holds up the skirt. Above this the woman wraps the third of her garments, another piece of cloth, which is tied around the waist and then folded over the left shoulder. This third piece can be used to carry a baby. Most women wear some form of headdress, either a scarf tied simply around the head or a more elaborately designed turban.

KOFI ANNAN

Kofi Annan, a Ghanaian, became internationally famous in 1997, when he was made the United Nations secretary-general. His term of office began with a crisis in Iraq, where UN weapons inspectors were in dispute with the Iraqi government over access to certain areas. Secretary-General Annan was able to defuse what might have developed into a very dangerous situation, as American and British troops were poised to attack Iraq.

Annan was a career official in the United Nations. He joined the World Health Organization (WHO) as a clerk in 1962, and after thirty years of service, he was nominated to its highest position. He was educated in the United States and Switzerland. His job at the United Nations came at a time of crisis for the world organization. The UN's role was no longer well defined in a post–Cold War era, and it was seriously in debt. About half the member states were not paying their contribution to its upkeep, including the United States, which owed over $1 billion. Kofi Annan served nine years as secretary-general, resigning in 2006.

INTERNET LINKS

https://www.cia.gov/library/Publications/the-world-factbook/geos /gh.html

The CIA World Factbook offers information about Ghana's population.

https://www.indexmundi.com/ghana/demographics_profile.html

Index Mundi provides information about the demographics of Ghana.

http://www.statsghana.gov.gh/socio_demo.html

This Ghanaian government site provides statistics about Ghana's population.

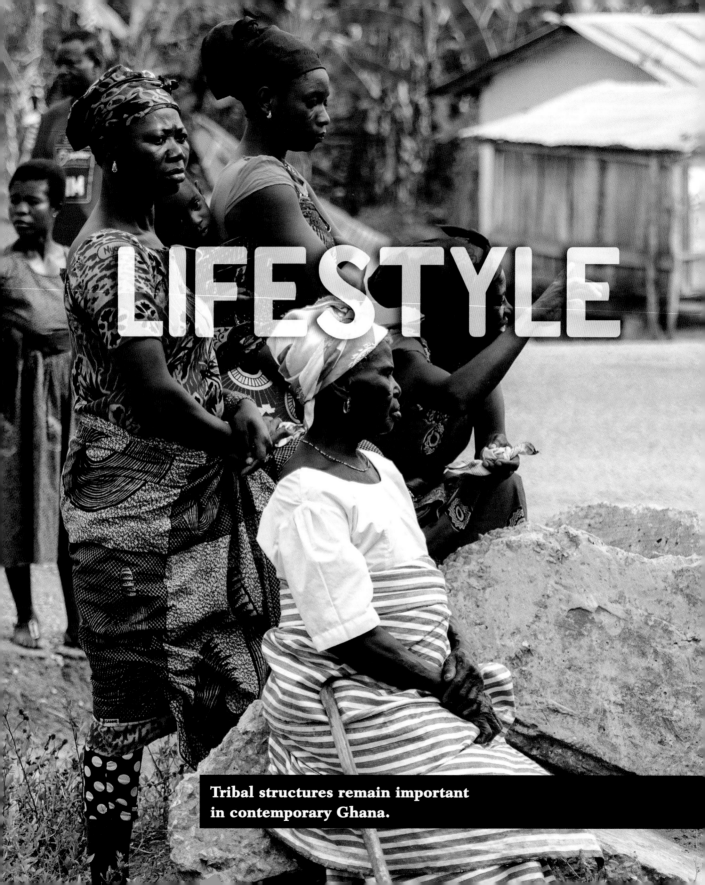

LIFESTYLE

Tribal structures remain important in contemporary Ghana.

7

THOSE IN GHANA'S SOUTHERN regions, who work in and benefit most from manufacturing and import-export, and who provide a home for Ghana's concentration of wealth, have adapted well to the stronger economy in recent years. Others are less well served. The majority of laborers in rural and mining regions lead hardscrabble lives and are late to receive the full benefits of Ghana's prosperity. In the far north, drought has caused poverty and malnutrition.

Ghana benefits from the presence of a number of international charities. ActionAid works in the north and is a source of loans, education, and health care. It also provides farmers with new seed. Aim Higher Africa, which was formed in 2013, focuses on improving education and encouraging entrepreneurs. The support of charities allows Ghana to continue improving life in ways it might not be able to attempt otherwise.

TRADITIONAL SOCIETY

The old tribal structures are still very important in rural areas. In the simplest unit of social structure, the nuclear family—father, mother, children—is usually headed by the man. He has responsibilities not only within his own nuclear and extended families—grandparents, aunts and uncles, cousins—but also in the village in which they all live—perhaps peacekeeping, organizing a festival, making sure spiritual observances are carried out, or looking after the water supply or sanitation. He forms part of the council of elders that advises the village chief on the running of the village.

In turn, the village chief sits on the council of elders of the divisional chief. A division might be a series of villages. Divisional chiefs advise the paramount chief, who is the highest authority in the clan. The paramount chief, like the lesser chiefs, inherits his position through his family, but he can be rejected by his people in favor of a relative if he turns out to be an ineffective leader. In the north of Ghana, the chief's symbol of power is an animal skin, while in the south it is a stool.

When chiefs gain office, they are said to be "enstooled" or "enskinned." If they are removed from office, they are "destooled" or "deskinned." Ordinary citizens can never become chief. Successive national governments have never sought to interfere with the chieftaincies. At the regional level, however, the paramount chiefs meet in a body set up by the government called the Regional House of Chiefs. Regional houses elect representatives to sit in a National House of Chiefs. When disputes between paramount chiefs occur, a judicial committee made up of chiefs and a high-court judge adjudicates.

Each paramount chief and his elders can make bylaws regarding traditional matters. They arbitrate on tribal matters, such as land tenure, inheritance, and custom. They are the essential core of all festivals that take place in Ghana. Although they have no legal role in local government matters, their disapproval of a new project or local government law would ensure that it did not happen. The paramount chiefs embody all that is best in their clans. On important occasions they wear beautiful ceremonial clothing and gold and silver jewelry.

FAMILY LIFE

The most common traditional family unit in Ghana is matrilineal, where a person is considered to be related to everyone on the mother's side of the family, including the mother's brothers, sisters, nieces, nephews, aunts, and uncles. In rural areas, the matrilineal family often lives in one compound or neighborhood and shares the land and property communally. Such an extended family would be called a clan. In Ghana, it is known as an *abusa* (ah-BOO-sah).

Less common are patrilineal families, where the family or clan is made up of those on the father's side. Included in the unit are the spirits of dead family members. At the head of the clan is the chief, the man who sits with the village elders and carries out the tribal duties. In a small village, all the residents may be from one family. When a chief is deposed or dies, all the sons of the women in his family of the next generation are potential candidates for his position. The mothers in the clan are thus important and powerful, especially the mother of the chief.

The clan system affects every aspect of the Ghanaian lifestyle. Land tenure is held by the family, so land is rarely sold. Every member of an abusa has equal rights to the resources of the clan; likewise, any individual's wealth belongs to their family. The clan system also affects how public works are carried out in villages. If a new well or schoolroom is needed, it will belong to the whole abusa. Everyone therefore lends a hand or, if they can, donates cash to the building project.

URBAN SOCIETY

The clan system is less conspicuous in urban areas. Many people have migrated to the towns, leaving behind their traditional groups. They now earn salaries and live in nuclear families. If they are able to save, they will use the money to put their children through school, buy household goods, or even purchase their own house. Their lingering ties to the clan may be their general sense of duty or sentimental associations, rather than shared ownership of property. Nuclear family size is small.

MARRIAGE TRADITIONS

The traditional Ghanaian concept of marriage is very different from the Western one. Arranging a marriage is one's father's responsibility, so when

Marriage ceremonies in Ghana differ from tribe to tribe.

the son chooses his life partner, he tells his father about his choice. His mother usually checks the suitability of the girl. She might ask neighbors about illnesses in the family and determine how closely related she is to her future husband.

If she is acceptable, the father begins negotiations. A cryptic message passes between the two fathers, and the girl's family members do their own check on the boy and his background. A message goes back if the boy is found acceptable, and the wedding plans begin. By this time, the boy's father will have made two cash gifts to the bride's family—one when he sent his preliminary message, called the "knocking fee," and another when the agreement was accepted. A third payment is the "bride wealth" when the girl is handed over. It is seen as evidence of matrimonial union.

The first two fees are negotiated by the bride's father and they become his, but the third fee is a "deposit" that must be handed back in the event of a divorce. Among some clans, other payments go to brothers, aunts, and other relatives to compensate for their loss. Often—for example, among the Grusi-speaking tribes in northern Ghana—payments are made with an animal.

The marriage ceremony itself, a meeting between the parents to formalize the relationship, may or may not include either bride or groom. Afterward, the bride is summoned to the groom's house along with her friends and relatives. At the groom's house are his relatives, friends, and musicians. A boisterous party takes place, and the girl then remains at her husband's house.

Among some ethnic groups, particularly the matrilineal ones, the girl and her husband often return to live at her own family home. Such is the case among the Fanti, an Akan tribe. Among some groups, polygamy is common. The Fulani, for example, often live in family units of a man and his several wives and their children. Some men may have two families in separate homes, with two sets of children, each living with their own mother's clan. Divorce is a matter of paying back to the groom's family the "bride wealth." Any goods that the husband gave to the wife's family need not be returned.

Ghanaian marriage traditions vary, depending on tribe, religion, and whether the individuals are urban or rural dwellers. Most, however, include some version of the "knocking," in which the husband-to-be, his father, and assorted friends and kin formally visit the bride's family to state the groom's interest, and to determine if the bride is interested and available, and with what conditions. The term "knocking" refers simply to knocking at the door like any good, polite guest.

Depending on how the inquiry proceeds, the bride's family may request time to perform due diligence. They will check into such issues as heritable disabilities, employment status, the reputation of the groom and his family in their own community, and suitability to the bride.

OFFSPRING

The clan system has greatly influenced family size. At one time, if a clan were to be strong, the next generation had to be large. In the past, each couple was encouraged to have as many children as possible. As many as thirteen births were common for each woman, although many of the babies did not survive. Tribal wars and slave raids claimed more children, and many others died from diseases such as malaria and river-borne diseases. Nowadays, with land becoming scarcer, more children means a smaller share for each member of the clan. Tribal wars have ended, the infant mortality rate has declined, education is expensive, and family planning is available. Tribal thought, therefore, focuses less on having many children and more on providing better for a few.

Even so, children are still seen as economic and social assets of the clan. In their work for the family, they repay the costs of their birth and upbringing. Children fetch water, sweep the yard, tidy the house, wash clothing, and help on the farm. Girls have the toughest workload—helping out on the farm, doing housework, and cooking for the family. Boys are treated more casually, being allowed time to play. In poor families, boys are expected to contribute to the family income. Besides using slingshots to fell birds, they might do some gardening for pay. The more enterprising boys might have a small business of their own at a market. If they can collect enough money, they can buy snacks and sell them at a profit. Children as young as six may scamper around at such jobs in the evening after school.

When children grow up, their obligation to their parents continues. If they have moved to the town, they are expected to send money home regularly. If they still live in the village, they must provide for their parents, including their funeral expenses.

DOMESTIC LIFE

The cities offer a variety of homes to suit different budgets. There are government housing projects, as well as developments of privately owned houses that would not seem out of place in an American city. The home of a typical city dweller is likely to have electricity, plumbing, good sanitation, and consumer appliances such as a TV set and a refrigerator. Western-style

A typical village home in Ghana

upholstered armchairs and carpets may fill the rooms. The wealthiest people in Ghana have lifestyles that are comparable to those of their counterparts in the West.

Some city districts, such as Nima in Accra, are slums or shantytowns. Those areas escaped town planning and have no piped water, electricity, or sanitation. Often, open sewers flow through the streets. In Accra, in 2009, some seven hundred thousand people had no access to sanitation. Many of those who live in the shantytowns are poor migrants who have no clan system to support them, no financial resources, and no patches of land to grow their food. They mostly live from hand to mouth.

In the countryside, the traditional house is built by its owner out of the cheapest available materials. No planning permits are required, nor are there rules about sanitation. A typical village house of someone who is fairly well-off has several rooms, including a kitchen, bathroom, living room, and veranda, where most of the day's activities take place.

Each parent may have their own bedroom, with shared rooms for young girls and individual rooms for teenage girls and each boy. Typical household furniture may include carved stools that are kept indoors, with some chairs and crude wooden stools outside. The bedrooms may have a simple wooden bed with a mattress and a sheet. Floors are covered in reed mats. Clothes and possessions are kept in chests. Children sleep on woven rush mats that are aired outdoors every day.

In the village, one may find a communal well, an elementary school, a church or mosque, perhaps a bar or café, and a few public buildings such as a mill, a dispensary and clinic, and a marketplace. Beyond the village are the fields, where animals graze and the crops are grown.

HEALTH AND SANITATION

Some parts of Ghana experience long periods of either torrential rain with flooding or severe drought. Water management thus is an important aspect of the nation's health care. About 15 percent of the rural population does not

A woman collects water at a village well.

have access to safe drinking water. Many people draw their water from a nearby river, which may be polluted by insecticides, the runoff from a factory upstream, or sewage and animal waste. Where complex water systems have been installed, such as piped water from a well, the local community may not have the means or skills to maintain it, and the supply is lost.

Most rural women in Ghana depend on traditional midwives for help in delivering their babies. Many local midwives nowadays have been trained in nutrition for expectant mothers, as well as basic hygiene. Charities, the churches, and the government have also set up clinics in many villages, where vaccination programs are carried out and rudimentary health care is provided. For more serious illnesses, people must travel to urban areas, where most of the government hospitals are located.

SCHOOLING

Students raise their hands in school.

Compared with many of its African neighbors, Ghana has a good educational system. At four years of age, a child's educational journey begins with two years of kindergarten. All children between ages six and twelve attend six years of free compulsory elementary education. In rural areas, facilities can be as humble as a shady spot under a tree. Often teachers are difficult to recruit for poor and remote locations. They are usually relocated from another part of Ghana and are not part of the local clan, so they may feel excluded and find life quite hard. For the first three years, children are taught in their mother tongue and English is taught as a second language. Subsequently, English becomes the official medium of instruction.

Coming of age is an important part of life for village children. It marks their arrival at adulthood and is celebrated by the whole village. It is usually incorporated into one of the festivals observed by the village.

Boys from the Fanti ethnic culture are given the uniform of their local militia. (The militia, in addition to combating crime in their communities, engages in social and economic activities to help promote community development.) The night before the festival, a bonfire is lit, and the teenage boys to be initiated and their fathers gather together. The boys are taught the secret stories of their militia, and purification rituals are carried out.

The Dipo puberty ceremony for girls of the Krobo group is more elaborate, with rituals varying according to the customs of the clan. Generally they follow the pattern that, on reaching puberty, girls are taken to the family compound and put on display for all the neighbors to see. In other ethnic groups, they walk around the streets, greeting the villagers. In some tribes, the girls wear very little besides beads. After this, there is an eight-day period when the girls are isolated and cannot touch anything associated with adult life, such as the stove, their newly bought clothes, or the gifts that their family and neighbors bring. At the end of this period of exclusion, the girls are dressed in their finest new clothes and are presented with gifts that form their capital and that remain their personal property even after marriage.

Circumstances are changing in regard to how many Ghanaians complete primary education and continue on to secondary. UNESCO figures as of 2016 indicate 93.14 percent of Ghanaian students successfully transfer from primary to secondary education. However, problems still remain in northern rural Ghana, where girls can become victims of poverty and social expectations. Ghana is making a serious effort to counter a continuing problem educating its rural population, and in particular its rural girls. Collaborating with UNESCO and other organizations, the Ghanaian government is working to give access to a population often presumed to have no future but to marry young and live in a domestic setting.

In addition to the state educational system, there are a number of private schools. An important feature of the government's efforts to establish literacy in the country is the mass education campaigns that make use of the radio to teach literacy, citizenship, health care, good farming practice, and house building.

Ghana has steadily improved the lives and fortunes of its children over the past thirty years, making huge dents in the dangers that were historically present. However, the nation still struggles to ensure all children are given sufficient food, medical care, education, and security.

INTERNET LINKS

https://www.commisceo-global.com/resources/country-guides/ghana-guide
Commisceo Global provides information on cultural norms in Ghana.

http://www.everyculture.com/Ge-It/Ghana.html
This website offers a summary of Ghanaian culture.

http://traveltips.usatoday.com/culture-ghana-africa-13608.html
This *USA Today* article provides information about Ghanaian culture.

RELIGION

Ghanaian Muslims pray in Accra's Independence Square.

GHANA IS A SECULAR STATE WITH A highly religious population. Almost all Ghanaians practice at least one religion. Many enjoy syncretist practices, blending and overlapping beliefs, rituals, and disciplines of Ghana's many religious traditions. In so complicated a religious environment, Ghana's government remains religiously neutral, favoring and furthering no one tradition over another.

Ghana's majority religions are Christianity, Islam, and animistic religions based on ancient tribal belief. Animism is indigenous to the region, with the deepest historical roots. Christianity and Islam are comparatively recent additions, but they have taken their place as central to Ghanaian cultures. Almost no one is entirely free of at least some traces of the ancient animistic religions. Tribal legends, stories, and beliefs color the thoughts and actions of even dedicated Christians and Muslims, as rooted in culture as Europeans who incorporated ancient pagan culture and faith even after their own conversion to Christianity.

The majority of Ghanaians are Christian, with a current standing of 71 percent. That includes 28 percent of the population that are Pentecostal/Charismatic, 18 percent that are Protestant, 13 percent that are Catholic, and 11 percent that belong to other Christian groups. Muslims constitute about 18 percent of the population. The majority of Ghanaian Muslims are

Sunni, though a significant number belong to the Ahmadiyyah and Tijaniyah sects of Sufi Islam. The remaining portion of Ghanaians are devoted to traditional tribal faith, to other imported religions, or are without formal faith.

TRADITIONAL FAITHS

Many religions are included in the term "animism" in Ghana. These religions share the common idea that there exists a spiritual world in which such inanimate things as trees, rocks, streams, or even the village well are imbued with life or spirit (animated) and are able to cause harm or bring good to people who come in contact with them. Consequently, all objects must be treated respectfully and appeased if necessary. They can also be called on for help, using a juju priest as an intermediary agent.

Most of Ghana's ethnic groups believe in three forms of spiritual power—the spirits of the things around them, the spirits of their ancestors, and a single god, Nyame, who created the world. The creator god is less important in the daily lives of the animist peoples than the other two. Ancestors are the most important aspect of one's spiritual life, and the recently deceased are the most powerful of all. If properly treated, the ancestors are benevolent. But they can be vengeful if they are slighted—for example, by an improperly conducted ritual.

SPIRITUAL HEALERS

A mixture of physician and priest, the juju priest mediates between his patients or believers and the spirits. Also known as the *abirifo* or *bayi okomfo*, his job is often hereditary, with the father passing his skills on to the son. Often the son will have given some sign of his inclination, perhaps by falling into a trance. The priest has a great assortment of natural herbs and remedies for all kinds of illnesses. Because he may believe that an illness is caused by some malevolent spirit, such as an irritated ancestor, part of his cure may be to appease that angry spirit and to wear a talisman as protection against it.

The animistic deity Anansi, the trickster spider, is reckoned as part of the Ashanti culture. During the slave diaspora, thousands of Ghanaians familiar with Anansi's stories were transported around the world, carrying the stories of their clever god with them. Now Anansi has become a world-striding figure, as familiar to many in today's Western cultures as their own ancestral gods.

He creates charms, potions, and incantations to protect his patients against evil spirits, curses, and other spiritual mishaps.

A talisman is made of items that are believed to hold magical power. Often they are made of animal bone or skin. The more powerful an object was in life, the more power it has to protect the victim, so often the talisman will be part of a tiger or some other powerful creature. To obtain help from the juju priest, the family and the suffering person must visit the priest, bringing gifts. The priest listens to their problems and then works his magic to the drumming, singing, and dancing of his assistant priests. The juju is well paid for his ministry.

The sick may seek out an *odunsini*, who is a spiritual herbalist with great knowledge of herbs and concoctions. The healer is trained to navigate the rituals necessary for obtaining the herbs without offending the gods.

The *bosomfo* or *okomfo* incorporates all the functions of the other healers while playing the role of attendant to the gods (represented in the form of a shrine). The Ashanti nation was formed by the priest Okomfo Anokye, who was believed to have received the golden stool from the heavens.

The Muslim religious healers in Ghana are called *malams*. They create talismans that contain quotes from the Quran and other writings, and herbs. These talismans are supposed to protect the wearer against evil spirits, bad luck, and diseases.

Ghanaians who follow tribal animistic traditions enjoy a pantheon of deities, from Nyame the creator god and Anansi the trickster, to their own ancestors, who become patrons in the afterlife, much as many Westerners believe their dead become angels or saints. These beliefs blend into the practices of both Christianity and Islam in Ghana.

AKAN FAITHS

The Akan people, who make up the largest group in Ghana, believe that a person is made up of three distinct spiritual and physical elements. Each person inherits their physical being, called the *mogya* (MOG-yah), or blood, from their mother, while their spiritual side, or *ntoro* (n-TORO), comes from the father. *Okra*, the soul, comes from Nyame, the creator god. This belongs to Nyame and returns to him after death. The Akan have their own calendar, which consists of nine cycles of forty days each, called *adae* (AHD-ay). In each cycle, there are two special days on which the tribe pays its respects to the spirits of the ancestors.

The Akan maintain the stools of past chiefs, believing that their spirits rest in the stools. So in each forty-day period, one day is set aside to honor the chiefs. The stool room is usually a sacred place that only the chief and the priests of the ancestors can enter. In some tribes, ordinary people are never allowed to see the stools, even when they are taken outside for purification rites. During the day of worship, the stools are visited by the chief and his attendants and are given food and drink, and the chief retells the stories of the ancestors' brave deeds.

The Ashanti golden stool has religious, political, and historical significance in the shaping of the Ashanti (also called Asante) nation and the identity of Ghana. The War for Independence, which began on March 28, 1900, was instigated by Yaa Asantewaa, a queen mother who mobilized the Ashanti troops to lay siege to the British mission at Fort Kumasi for three months. The British governor, Lord Hodgson, had demanded that the Ashanti turn over to the British Empire the golden stool that was the throne and a symbol of the Ashanti struggle for

In the Ashanti religion, the supreme deity is called Nyame. Beneath him is a pantheon of lesser gods embodied by the earth's physical features, such as the Tano River, Nyame's favorite son. Below them are even smaller gods, or abosom (ah-BOH-som)—objects of spiritual power. While Nyame is so remote that he cannot be appealed to, the abosom are ready to help if appealed to in the right way. All over Ghana, abosom houses exist where the abosom are worshipped and addressed as if they were elders of the clan. Inside an abosom house is a brass basin containing the essential elements of the abosom—perhaps some river mud, herbs, beads, shells, or other revered objects. The abosom can enter into the body of a priest if it so wishes.

independence. To force out information on where the golden stool was hidden, children and their parents were bound and beaten by the British, who had to bring in several thousand troops to break the siege.

The British troops also plundered villages, confiscated Ashanti lands, and killed many people. Queen Yaa Asantewaa was exiled to the Seychelles Islands, while most of the captured chiefs became prisoners of war. Yaa Asantewaa died twenty years later in exile. Today, the Seat of State that is used ceremonially by the president of Ghana takes the form of the Akan stool. It was first used in 1960 when Ghana became a republic.

GHANAIAN CHRISTIANITY

The first Christians to come to Ghana were the Portuguese, who introduced Roman Catholicism in the fifteenth century. They made little effort to convert the local people, so Christianity did not take root until the second half of the nineteenth century, when missionary societies began to set up churches and schools.

THE SUPREME BEING

An Akan story tells how the supreme creator, Nyame, got into the sky. In the very earliest days, the creator lived close to man, on the rooftops of the houses. One day he was passing some old women pounding fufu (FOO-foo), a doughy mixture of cassava and plantains. The harder the women pounded, the farther Nyame bounced into the sky, until eventually he reached the highest heavens and decided to stay there. But by then he was no longer close to the people that he created, so he had to call on the tallest things to talk to his people for him. That is how people learned to worship the high things, such as mountains and trees, which were close to Nyame and could easily carry messages yet farther up to him. When the Ashanti create altars to Nyame, it is always in the shape of a tree with a fetish figure sitting in it. When a drum maker or boat builder cuts down a tree to make his drum or boat, he always appeases the tree because of its mighty power to intercede between him and the supreme being, Nyame.

A Methodist church in Accra

The Basel Missionary Society started missionary work in Ghana in 1828. The Wesleyan Methodists arrived in the 1830s, led by Thomas Birch Freeman. He was half-African and went to the Ashanti region to set up his mission. By 1843, the Wesleyans had twenty-one missions in Ghana. In 1876, they founded the first secondary school in the country. Farther inland, Bremen missions were established east of the Volta, working with the Ewe people. That fellowship later became the modern Evangelical Presbyterian Church of Ghana.

In the early years of the twentieth century, many Ghanaians were converted to Christianity because of the work of William Wadé Harris, a Liberian who traveled across West Africa and whose teachings were so persuasive that he was deported from Côte d'Ivoire. Although he was an American Episcopalian missionary, he helped to convert thousands of people from animism to Methodism, Roman Catholicism, and Anglicanism. His followers in Ghana set up their own new church, called the Church of the Twelve Apostles. Other Christian churches in Ghana include the Presbyterian, Evangelical, Baptist, African Methodist, and Episcopal Zion churches.

AFRICAN SPIRITUAL CHURCHES

The churches that arrived in Ghana in the eighteenth and nineteenth centuries appealed to people because of their similar ideas of a single creator god and also because of their efforts to educate local people. But the nonnative churches all lacked an African flavor. Over the years, indigenous churches that mixed the belief in a forgiving savior with the high spirits and enthusiasm of African cultural life began to spring up all across West Africa.

One of those churches was the Church of the Lord, Aladura. That began among the Yoruba people of Nigeria and was based on the ideas of an American church, the Faith Tabernacle Church of Philadelphia, which practiced faith healing and the laying on of hands. In 1918, a horrendous worldwide influenza epidemic killed many people in West Africa, and a prayer group within the Anglican Church started to practice faith healing in an effort to save lives from the viral onslaught.

Priests and healers are important parts of African Christian practices.

By the 1920s, that sect had been forced out of the Anglican Church, but it had become very popular and spread from its home in Nigeria across West Africa, establishing a branch called the Christ Apostolic Church in Ghana. Later churches came to be called Aladura churches and practiced even more occult forms of Christianity, featuring prophets who claimed they could foretell the future, heal the sick, and even make amulets for protection, just as the juju priests did. Often these amulets included inscriptions from the Bible rather than fragments of animal bone. Prayer meetings are often very lively, with singing, African-style drumming, and street processions.

In Ghana, the most important days in the Christian calendar are Christmas and Good Friday.

Ghana's ancient animistic religions are, in many instances, the closest most Westerners come to an understanding of African religions. Because such a large portion of the slave diaspora came from the Gold and Ivory Coasts, it was those traditions that made their way into the world beyond. They continued in various forms, ranging from fairly accurate representations of the original traditions, through adapted versions such as Vodun and Candomblé, to the outright caricatures of traditional religion most people in the United States are familiar with—"voodoo" rich with sexy priestesses, terrifying demons, zombies, and mind-altering drugs.

Traditional animistic Ghanaian religion, like many similar tribal religions, works on a belief in a world drenched in spiritual potential. In this world, places are sacred or accursed, and animals are spiritual kin to mankind and sometimes are minor gods or guides. Ancestors serve as patron spirits, protecting their friends and family but exerting negative influence on those who cross them. Priests, both men and women, can intercede with this powerful, spirit-haunted world, serving as diplomats to the gods and spirits.

Entire pantheons of gods and powers exist in these traditions. Figures as diverse as Nyame, Anansi, Oyo, and others interact with humankind, for good or ill. Westerners tend to see much of this as alien and peculiar, seldom taking time to see that their own traditions are not so different, with supernatural figures including deities, angels, saints, the sacred dead, and ranks of demons all creating as complex and spirit-haunted a secondary world as that of the animistic religions.

GHANAIAN ISLAM

Islam arrived in Ghana with Arab traders taking gold to Sudan, probably sometime around the seventeenth century. It is more popular among the peoples in northern Ghana, although there are clusters of Muslims throughout the country. Most Fulani, Mamprusi, Dagomba, and some Ashanti have become Muslims.

Islam originated in Arabia in the seventh century and follows the teachings of the prophet Muhammad. Muslims believe in one God, in angels who bring the word of God to the people, and in a number of prophets before Muhammad who received God's message. One of those prophets, they believe, was Jesus. Other prophets are Abraham, Moses, and the writers of the New Testament, all figures that are part of Christianity. Muslims also believe in the final day of judgment, when they will hear the trumpet of the angel Asrafil. The main form of Islam practiced in Ghana is Sunni Islam, but there is another sect, called the Ahmadiyyah, a Sufi faction considered heretical by most other Muslims, which has converts in southern Ghana. That sect recognizes another prophet after Muhammad, a man called Mirza Ghulam Ahmad, who lived in India and claimed to be the *mahdi* (MAH-dee), the figure who was to appear at the end of the world. He also claimed to be the reincarnation of Christ and of the Hindu god Krishna. In Ghana, the sect is represented by the Telemul Islam Ahmadiyyah Movement, which has its headquarters in Saltpond. A proselytizing sect, it runs several secondary schools and is happy to convert people to any form of Islam, not just its own.

INTERNET LINKS

http://academic.depauw.edu/mkfinney_web/teaching/Com227 /culturalPortfolios/GHANA/WorldViewReligion.html
This DePauw University article provides information on the religions practiced in Ghana.

http://www.globalreligiousfutures.org/countries/ghana
The Pew-Templeton Religious Futures Project examines the varied religions in Ghana.

https://www.modernghana.com/news/440155/traditional-african -religion-still-very-relevant.html
This news article explores how important traditional African religion remains in Ghana today.

LANGUAGE

There are approximately one hundred indigenous languages in Ghana in addition to English.

9

GHANA, A NATION OF approximately one hundred indigenous languages, is unified by its acceptance of English, a foreign import, as its official language and lingua franca. The choice to make English the official language of government, education, and trade places all other native languages on an even footing. It also opens the door to trade and tourism by ensuring that the nation shares a working knowledge of English with much of the rest of the developed world.

Not all Ghanaians are equally fluent, though. While all Ghanaians are exposed to English in school and in public life, many—particularly many rural poor—are limited to the local creole of English, native languages, and creative and innovative bridges between the two. Just as most "traditional" English speakers find Jamaican or Cajun creoles hard to understand, most struggle to follow Ghanaian English creoles.

Hausa, a Nigerian language, serves as a secondary lingua franca, being used for most intertribal communications.

Most people are able to speak at least on lingua franca to a level that is useful in their daily life. For some, that means very little beyond a few working phrases. For more, it means native-level proficiency in a creole version in addition to native fluency in their own tribal language.

"If we can really start to understand that we are African people, then we can go beyond just looking at the Western languages of our colonial enemies and western languages of our villages to actually learning other African languages. And when we do that, we will be building African collectiveness."
—Dr. Obadele Kambo

The Ashanti people use traditional adinkra symbols, such as these, to convey words, sayings, or concepts.

Common tribal languages include Akan dialects, Ewe, Ga, and Dagbani.

All students are exposed to basic English in the first two years of compulsory education. The levels of teaching skill, however, vary extremely throughout the country, and the access to advanced teaching is highly dependent on both schools and on student interest and access.

AKAN FAMILY

Most of the people who live along the coast and in the southern regions of Ghana speak an Akan language. Akan dialects are very close, and speakers of those dialects can communicate quite well. The vocabulary is the same in most dialects, with differences only in pronunciation and accent. For comparison, think of the difficulty of communication between an American and someone with a heavy Scottish or Australian accent.

That means that people from the south coast can understand other speakers living as far away as the Black Volta, Lake Volta, or the border with Côte d'Ivoire, although the language they speak may be called Ashanti, Fanti, Akuapem, or any one of tens of other names. Because each language or dialect has a different written form, they remain separate languages.

GUR FAMILY

The people in northern Ghana speak one of three forms of the Gur language—Dagbani, Grusi, and Gurma. None of those languages is spoken or understood in the south of the country, except by the few people from the north who have migrated south to Accra or one of the other coastal towns. Dagbani is the most widely spoken branch of the Gur language. It includes the dialects spoken in the Nankansi, Gurensi, Dagbon, Mamprusi, and Talensi-Kusasi regions. Those languages are not as mutually comprehended as the Akan dialects. Neighboring groups understand one another, but groups that live any distance apart cannot. Because of that, Dagbani, the language spoken in the Dagbon region, has become a lingua franca. When northern speakers and southern speakers meet, however, they almost always communicate in English, which has become another lingua franca. Thus, northern Ghanaians know their own language and usually the language of their nearest neighbors, as well as Dagbani as the northern lingua franca and English as the national lingua franca.

WRITING

All Ghanaian languages existed only in a spoken form until the missionaries arrived in West Africa. In order to bring the message of the Bible to the local people, missionaries set out to learn the local languages and devise a written script for them. Because many of the missionaries who learned and transcribed the languages were linguists, they often wrote the dialects in the orthography of linguistics—inventing symbols representing sounds. Thus, all over Ghana today public signs and notices written in local languages have some characters that are not in the Roman alphabet.

Not all Ghanaian languages have a written system. Languages in which teaching materials are being developed for use in high schools and colleges and for use in the media are Akan, Dagaare-Wali, Dagbani, Adangme, Ewe, Ga, Gonja, Kasem, and Nzema. Another important written language is Arabic. Most Muslim children attend a *makaranta* (Islamic school) where they learn to read and write Arabic.

ENGLISH IN GHANA

A native speaker of English who arrives in Ghana and stands on the street listening may have considerable difficulty recognizing his own language being spoken. Not only is the accent different, the way words are strung together (syntax) is also different. Many African languages are tonal, meaning that the tone of the speaker's voice alters the meaning of the word, just as in Chinese dialects. Some Ghanaians have applied such a tonal system to English.

Ghana has three national newspapers—*Daily Graphic, Ghanaian Times,* and the *Daily Guide*—and fifteen or so other regular newspapers. There is considerable freedom of the press today, although in the recent past this was not the case.

SPOKESMEN

Among many of the tribes of Ghana, an important member of the chief's entourage is the okyeame *(otch-ee-AH-mee), or spokesman. He accompanies the chief on all his official duties and carries a special symbol of office, a mace. His job is to listen to what the chief says and translate it for the people, even if the chief and his people speak the same language. He spends his apprenticeship learning how to say things in the most euphemistic and flattering way.*

For everything that the chief wants to say, there is a polite and diplomatic way of saying it. The chief merely concentrates on the substance of his message, while the spokesman retells it for him in a literary and decorative way. The spokesman may not add any new information to the chief's words, but he can refer back to ancient stories or create a beautiful image. He polishes the chief's words for him. Among some tribes, the spokesman also mediates between the chief and his subjects. The chief whispers to the spokesman what he wants to say, and the spokesman makes the chief's words fit into a selection of well-known proverbs.

Another difficulty English speakers might encounter is unfamiliar vocabulary. In the United States and Britain, some of the vocabulary has changed over the years, moving the two usages of English apart. That has happened in Ghana, too, where some older English words are still used together with new words from local languages or invented words. Other familiar English words have taken on new meanings. For example, the word "dash" has joined the Ghanaian form of English and means "to give." Originally a Portuguese word, it has replaced the word "give" in local English.

The word "sister" is used more widely than in American or British English. In Ghana, it can be used as a friendly form of address to any young woman; for example, school friends would call each other sister. Another expression is "my dear." In American English, it is a way of being friendly to someone. In Ghanaian English, it means girlfriend or boyfriend. Someone might therefore say, "I saw your my dear at church this morning," meaning "I saw your boyfriend." In British English, calling someone an "old crow" is a term of abuse, but in Ghanaian English it is a compliment, meaning that the person is wise.

In some cases, Ghanaian English has become almost a new language, known as pidgin English, with not only its own vocabulary but a different grammar system based on local languages. Often the verbs "is" or "have" are left out and the letter "s" is left off the ends of words. In other cases, the word is repeated to make a plural. In many regions, teachers find it easier to teach their pupils in the local pidgin version of English for the first few years and then move on to standard English in the senior years. Since many children do not go beyond elementary school, pidgin English is the only form they learn. Generally, the longer a student has been in school, the closer his or her English will be to that understood and used in the United States or Britain.

ADAGES AND TALES

Much of Ghanaian folk wisdom is conveyed in a vast trove of proverbs that are well known to everyone in the country. The proverbs—moral tales that teach the values of the family and clan—are told to children again and again.

In Ghana, mammy wagons, or public transportation vans, are known by the slogans that are painted on them.

Like many other countries in West Africa, Ghana has a tradition of talking drums. These are drums that are used as a means of communication rather than for making music. They are hourglass-shaped, with skins stretched over both ends and joined by tightly drawn rawhide cords. As the cords are stretched or released by the drummer, the tone of the beaten drum changes, precisely following the tonal pattern of the language that it is copying.

In the days before telephones, the drummers of talking drums learned to beat out messages like a kind of Morse code, but the sounds that the drum made actually copied the sounds of the words they conveyed. Those drums are used today for ceremonial purposes, where once they relayed important messages across hundreds of miles.

They are often written or drawn on everyday objects. Mammy wagons (vans used for public transportation), for example, always have some message or drawing painted on the front. Sometimes such aphorisms as "The Lord is my shepherd" or "God is good" are taken from Christian or Muslim texts. More cryptic messages, written in English or a local language, might be "Poor no friend," meaning poverty is no friend to people. Both van drivers and their vans are known by their slogans.

Moral tales include stories about the naughty spider Anansi. He is part human and part spider and is very wicked. He tries to cheat people but always turns out to be too clever for his own good. The stories about him are fun to hear, and they teach children to be honest and well behaved.

NAMING TRADITIONS

In southern Ghana, people are named after the day on which they were born. This means that there are only fourteen possible names: seven men's names—Kwajo (Monday), Kwabena, Kwaku, Yaw, Kofi, Kwame, and Kwesi—and seven women's names—Adjoa, Abena, Akua, Yaa, Efua, Ama, and Esi. Thus Kofi Annan was born on a Friday, while Kwame Nkrumah was born on a Saturday.

In addition, each child is given a name chosen by his or her father, usually the name of a particularly respected ancestor. When two children in the same family are born on a same day, they will be given a number, too, so brothers both born on Friday will be called Kofi and Kofi Manu (second Kofi).

Other ways of naming a child might be to give a name that recalls some feature of their birth. An unexpected child born on Friday would be named Kofi Nyamekye (God given). A child born after the loss of a previous baby might be called Ababio (the returned one), meaning that the dead child has returned in the body of the new baby. In addition to those two names, there might be others, depending on the parents' wishes.

Many people in the cities also take Christian names, so people have a minimum of three names and a maximum of ten or more. Children are not given the first names of their parents at all, so within a family everyone's names are completely different unless they were born on the same day!

INTERNET LINKS

http://apics-online.info/contributions/16
Linguists offer information about Ghanaian English on this site.

https://www.ethnologue.com/country/gh/languages
This website features an alphabetized list of Ghanaian languages, with descriptions.

https://www.timeout.com/accra/things-to-do/a-guide-to-ghanaian -slang-dialect
This *TimeOut* article examines Ghanaian pidgin.

ARTS

The Ashanti people were traditionally known
for crafting beautiful objects out of gold.

10

GHANA DOES NOT OFFER A CLEAR line of distinction between festivals, rituals, arts, crafts, traditional cultural activities, modern entertainments, and other behaviors that most modern Westerners think justify specific labels. These various activities flow into each other in a variety of ways and have evolved together based on the domestic and spiritual needs of the Ghanaian people.

Ghanaian traditional arts and crafts have a long history, both within rural tribes and African tribal empires. Drawing from the art of ancient Benin, Ghanaian art is created and appreciated not only for aesthetic purposes but as historical and ritualistic objects. Westerners who are not aware of this might lose out on comprehending its full meaning.

Ghana's modern participation in the arts is not negligible. Current landmark artists and performers in the Ghanaian art scene include the painter Jeremiah Quarshie and the writer Taiye Selasi.

MUSIC

Music is an integral part of Ghanaian life and culture. When a folk story is performed, it is usually accompanied by music, using either traditional instruments or more modern sounds. Music and singing accompany a Ghanaian's life from daily work to such major life events as birth, puberty,

"I'm an artist who is given to working with materials in my environment. I think all the things that were taught in art school I set about subverting them ... Using plaster of Paris and such things which are imported—you know, they don't make plaster in Ghana. So it means that you do art with whatever is around you."

—El Anatsui, Ghanaian sculptor

and funerals. Most traditional music is played on four types of instruments—idiophones, such as rattles and xylophones, that would vibrate naturally; membranophones, such as drums; aerophones, such as horns and pipes; and chordophones, various types of stringed instruments.

The many musical instruments in Ghana have different uses within the various ethnic groups. Among some tribes, their use is restricted to particular religious events or may be played only for certain chiefs. The *nkofe* (n-KOFF-eh) horns may be played by the chief of the Ashanti clan, while the *kikaa* (KEE-kah) horn is used only in the Dagbon region and for praise songs about the divisional chiefs. Another example is the *apirede* (ap-eer-EH-deh) ensemble, made up of several drums, a gong, and clappers, which can be played only by the men whose job is to carry the royal stools of the chiefs.

Some drums are thought to imitate the cries of specific animals. One makes the ominous noise of a leopard, while another mimics a crocodile. They are played by tribes that regard those animals as totems.

Drums are important ritual and religious objects in Ghana.

A dilemma facing African writers is whether to write in their mother tongue or to write in the language of colonial times. The latter would take their work to a larger world audience but carries with it painful echoes of the colonial past. On the other hand, writing in the mother tongue restricts most Ghanaian writers to an audience of no more than half their country's population.

One of the drums known as talking drums, the *atumpan* (at-UM-pan) of the Akan people, mimics the tonal language of the people. It is a sacred drum and can be made only by certain clan craftsmen. A drummer himself must never make his own drum. The drum is made from a specific tree, and the membrane is made from the ear of an elephant. The pegs that hold the membrane down are also made from a special tree. The variable tones of the drum are created by stretching or relaxing the pegs that hold down the membrane. The drum is played with a hammer often made from an elephant's tusk. This type of drum was once used to "telegraph" messages across great distances, but its use is more ceremonial and cultural today.

MUSICAL STYLES

The modern music of the Ashanti people is called palm wine. It is solo guitar music that originated in the small bars and drinking spots of southern Ghana. The singer plays an acoustic guitar and improvises songs on the spot about the customers or about politics. The songs are often uncomplimentary and can be hilarious.

Highlife, a popular music style that blends many Ghanaian influences with foreign pop styles, including jazz, has been popular in Ghana since the 1930s. Highlife originated in the port towns of southern Ghana in the late nineteenth and early twentieth centuries. It is a fusion of traditional drumming and European-style tunes. This kind of music gained international popularity in the 1950s after Ghanaian musicians such as E. T. Mensah discovered American jazz during World War II. Mensah formed a professional dance band like the big bands of 1940s America, but his style was uniquely African, with powerful rhythms. In the 1950s, many such bands were popular.

Another important figure of the time was King Bruce, who played saxophone and trumpet and led the Black Beats, a band of some twenty musicians. He wrote songs in English and Ga. His career continued into the 1990s, and his songs were put onto CDs in 1997. Many more bands and individuals have found fame in Europe and the United States, notably Osibisa, Highlife International, Kantata, and Pat Thomas. The most popular highlife musician in the 1990s was Alex Konadu.

From the 1990s on, a new form of Ghanaian music evolved from highlife, called hiplife. Hiplife combines traditional Ghanaian music with hip-hop and has become very popular in West Africa and abroad. Popular hiplife musicians include Hammer of the Last Two, Samini, Edem, and Sarkodie.

Since 2000, the Ghanaian music industry has organized the Ghana Music Awards to appreciate and reward musicians who have excelled in the main music genres of Ghana, including gospel, hiplife, highlife, reggae, and traditional.

TRADITIONAL DANCE

Like much of Ghanaian art, dance plays a large part in the lives of ordinary people. It is an ancient tradition, and each movement of the dancer often expresses a symbolic as well as social meaning. The dances of the various ethnic groups are each different in style and in purpose. Particular movements are typical of the different clans. The Akans, for example, use complex footwork, coordinated with intricate hand and body movements. The dances of the Frafra are much simpler and are performed by columns of line dancers moving in synchronization and concentrating on foot stamping, with few hand or body movements except swaying.

The Dagomba often incorporate stooping and leaping movements into their dances, while in northern Ghana the dances are more acrobatic, with tumbling and lifting. The dances of men and women also vary, with women's dancing being more sinuous and men's more angular and sharp. Individual movements convey symbolic meanings for the spectators. Reaching up to the sky indicates a call to God, while rolling the wrists together and drawing them sharply apart indicates the breaking of chains, or the freedom of the dancer. Mime often enters into the performances of the dances. Funeral dances are usually solemn and slow, while birth, puberty, and wedding dances are faster and more exhilarating.

TEXTILES AND STOOLS

The most famous artifacts of Ghana are kente cloth and the gold weights and stools of the Ashanti chiefs. Among many groups, cloth for clothing is a printed cotton, but among the Ashanti, the cloth is woven in strips with intricate designs and is very valuable. Traditionally, kente cloth was woven only by men, although a few women have now learned the skill. In the nineteenth century, weavers began buying silk thread from European traders and weaving it into the designs. The woven motifs are geometric, and each weaver has his own style. The Ashanti chiefs have their own royal weavers, who make cloth for the chiefs and their mothers. Each color and geometric design has its own meaning. Gold and yellow signify God, royalty, eternal life, and prosperity. White represents purity and joy, while green is newness and fertility. Red stands for death, so plain red outfits are worn at family funerals. Blue represents both love and the power of the queen mothers. Circles show the presence of God, triangles fertility and womanhood, and rectangles virility and manhood.

A Ghanaian dance ensemble performs in a street festival.

Adinkra is a main ceremonial cloth for most Ghanaians in the south. It has stamped patterns and symbols important to the Ghanaians and is worn for sad occasions. According to Ashanti legend, it was introduced in 1818 following the capture of a rival monarch, named Adinkra, who wore the cloth to express his sorrow on being taken to Kumasi. Adinkra designs are printed in a black dye made from the bark of certain trees, using stamps carved from sections of calabash wood.

Ancestral stools are another art form whose significance is far more than artistic in Ghanaian society. In some villages in central and southern Ghana, parents have a stool made for each of their children, and the stool comes to represent the child's life energy. People keep their own stool all their life, and when they die, their body is seated on the stool while it is prepared for burial. After death, the stool is placed in the ancestral huts and is venerated by the family as the actual spirit of the deceased.

The stools are made of three pieces—a rectangular base, a seat that is curved like a barrel stave, and a carved supporting pillar or pillars between them, where the importance and character of the owner is described. For a wealthy chief or a rich man, the stool is intricately carved. In all cases, the symbolism of the carvings is important. Some stools are plated with silver or, in the case of the early Ashanti kings, with gold. After death, each person's stool is treated with egg yolk, soot, and sheep's blood, symbolizing peace and caution. Stool carvers are craftsmen and religious figures. When the wood for a stool is cut, religious rituals are performed.

Another art form that is also part of tribal religious beliefs is the carving of wooden figures. These may be kept in totem or fetish houses, where they either represent the animist gods or become intermediaries between the people and the animist gods. An infertile woman might carry a carved wooden doll on her back that would transmit her wish for children and may bring help from the animist spirits. Other such dolls may be placed around houses or on the outskirts of the village to protect the tribe. The dolls represent each tribe's vision of beauty and may be scarified or carved to represent the fertility of a woman or the angular qualities of men.

COFFINS AS ART

Funerals are lavish and expensive affairs in Ghana. The more important the deceased, the more elaborate their funeral. In recent years, an unusual art form has developed around the funerals of some Ghanaians, where coffin makers are commissioned to make a coffin that depicts the occupation of the deceased.

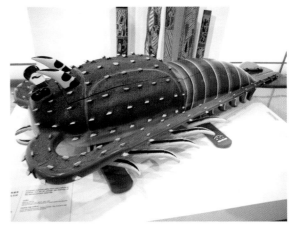

Thus a fisherman's coffin might be a huge tuna fish carved out of wood and painted, while a truck driver's coffin might be a small replica of the truck he drove. A pineapple farmer might be buried in a pineapple-shaped coffin, while a rich man might be buried in a model of a Cadillac automobile. People often commission their coffins long before they die since the work on each coffin is elaborate and may take many months. If the customer dies before his coffin is completed, the funeral is delayed until it is ready. Not surprisingly, these coffins are very expensive.

ARCHITECTURE

Ghana maintains an interesting architectural showcase of centuries-old castles and forts built by the Portuguese and British, modern buildings erected since the 1960s, and the indigenous building styles of the various ethnic groups.

Nothing remains of the city built by the Ashanti at Kumasi except some engravings. The last wars of the Ashanti against the British forces led to the sacking of the city. The engravings show complex structures built around central courtyards. Walls, doors, and shutters were intricately carved and, in the case of palaces, were covered in hammered silver or gold leaf. A royal pavilion has been reconstructed at the cultural center in Kumasi, showing what such a building would have been like.

GHANAIAN BRONZE WORK

Ghanaian artists have retained the ancient skills of lost-wax bronze casting. The Ashanti observed the method and incorporated it into their own work, where it is still in use to this day.

Lost-wax casting is the art of creating an initial form for jewelry or sculpture using wax. The image is sculpted in wax, and around it is built an encasing mold with an inlet to let in molten bronze. The bronze enters the mold, melting away the wax, which flows away, leaving a hollow place for the bronze to fill. This hollow left by the melted wax is the key to the lost-wax technique.

Contemporary Ghanaian artists continue to use the lost-wax technique to create different artistic forms. From traditional representations of the animistic tribal gods to refined, sleek modern sculptures and jewelry, Ghana continues to produce elegant bronze work.

Modern rural buildings are far more humble. In the south, buildings are square, often built around a central courtyard, and have a corrugated iron roof. At the entrance to the compound is a loggia, or roofed gallery, where guests are greeted. The walls are made of dried mud and are constantly reconstructed and decorated by the women who live in the house.

In the villages of the north, a series of circular huts is built around a central courtyard. Roofs are pointed and thatched. In the far north, roofs are terraced and form flat surfaces for drying crops or for the family to sleep on during hot weather. The walls are clay or unfired earth and are decorated either with paint or with designs etched into the drying mud. The buildings are often simple, with a kitchen area opening onto a courtyard and several sleeping rooms.

In the cities, domestic architecture is Western in style. The bungalows of richer people have yards and a parking space for their car. Public housing consists of apartment buildings in various stages of modernity.

LITERATURE

The earliest form of literature in Ghana was oral literature—the stories told over and over again by professional storytellers, who added to and updated the stories each time they were narrated. The stories would be told at special events, such as weddings, funerals, or other traditional ceremonies, and accompanied by guitar, percussion music, and singing. Storytelling often formed the means by which the values of the extended family or clan were passed on to the next generation.

A Ghanaian grandfather reads to his granddaughter.

Atukwei Okai (*center*) was one of Ghana's most prominent writers. He passed away in July 2018.

As tribal life gives way to modern city life, there is a fear that the old stories will be lost. Some of that oral tradition is being revitalized today, however, by performers such as Koo Nimo (Daniel Amponsah), who broadcasts modern versions of the ancient stories on Ghanaian radio. He maintains the moral and cultural aspects of the stories he tells, but like his predecessors, he updates the stories to bring in modern politics and issues.

Today, many Ghanaian writers have gained recognition as novelists, poets, and playwrights. Some successful Ghanaian writers are Christina Ama Ata Aidoo, Atukwei Okai, Asiedu Yirenkyi, and Ayi Kwei Armah, who wrote the powerful novel *The Beautiful Ones Are Not Yet Born*, about life in a newly independent African country. Christina Ama Ata Aidoo is one of a small number of female African writers and has written *The Dilemma of a Ghost* and *Anowa*.

SYMBOLS

Symbolism is an important part of the lives of Ghanaians. It can be seen in the design of kente cloth, in the patterns on the walls of huts, and in many other art forms. The chief's garments and jewelry are not just adornments. Each piece depicts a story of the chief's origins, his wealth, and the history of the clan. These symbols can be seen in other artifacts of Ghanaian life, such as on canoes, mammy wagons, ornamental gourds, stools, and cooking utensils.

A chameleon symbolizes a mixture of slowness and quickness, as well as the impermanence of words, which can change just like the chameleon's colors. A snail and a tortoise together symbolize the desire for peace, since neither of those creatures is ever hunted or shot at. A human figure holding its ear and pointing to its eye indicates that blindness does not prevent understanding in other ways. All of these symbols carved onto domestic items remind the owners of popular Ghanaian proverbs that express maxims to live by with propriety and laughter.

INTERNET LINKS

http://www.ghanamotion.com
You can stream Ghanaian music on this website.

https://theculturetrip.com/africa/ghana/articles/10-of-ghanas -best-contemporary-artists
This article looks into ten of Ghana's best contemporary artists.

https://www.youtube.com/watch?v=rVWsWNo6ji8&list=PLULEfTL6 1wpGNb-F8oZJLdHy6ga05m4a1
This video features a compilation of Ghanaian music videos.

LEISURE

People enjoy the water at Anomabo Beach.

11

GHANA'S PEOPLE ENJOY MANY leisure activities, and are fond of music, dancing, and parties with good companions. Festivals are commonly celebrated in the country, along with clan celebrations and seasonal events. From festivals to harvests to special events, there are always occasions for community gatherings. Urban residents still celebrate some festivals and holidays, but they have streamlined the complicated patterns of clan and tribal celebrations. Instead, they enjoy clubs, dance halls, theaters, and simple street celebrations, as well as the hustle and bustle of the market and daily social interactions in churches, taverns, and other urban venues.

"Little by little, even as we drink we make plans."
—Ghanaian proverb about constant purpose even when seemingly at rest

A concert party is a typical form of entertainment in Ghana's cities.

URBAN LEISURE

Most of the larger cities are in the south of Ghana, where the tourism industry is based. Accra has a flourishing nightlife, with many bars and music clubs that offer live music. A typical form of entertainment in the city is a concert party, which includes a play, a stand-up comic act, and music, while the audience drinks *akpeteshe* (ak-pet-ESH-ee), distilled palm wine. Ghana is the home of highlife music, an African big band sound that uses Western instruments and traditional drumming to produce African rhythms. In the large cities, that hybrid music is enjoyed at concert parties and in the churches, where a form of gospel highlife has developed.

Accra has nearly fifty churches in its city center alone. Churches are the heart of social life for many people, and on Sundays music and joyous singing can be heard in many of them, especially the indigenous African ones. Other favorite meeting places include food stalls and "chop houses," inexpensive café-style places found all around the cities. European and Asian restaurants are also found in the city centers. Movie theaters are popular, with African and Western films vying for popularity with kung fu movies. Ghana has a national theater, where local patrons and tourists can enjoy cultural shows and contemporary theater productions.

The St. Sylvanus Church choir, based near Accra, sings during a service.

RURAL LEISURE

In rural areas, leisure often takes second place to the grueling demands of the farming year. Leisure is more closely related to the festivals and traditions of the African religions than to the spare time or available cash of the people who

Women sell yams at the 2016 Gushiegu Potato Festival.

Radios remain important sources of news for many Ghanaians.

live in the villages. Because so many rural people live at a subsistence level, leisure is found only in activities that also benefit the family group. If they find spare time after the harvest or early in the season while the crops are growing, men will go out and hunt small animals.

In the countryside, many villages do not yet have a permanent supply of electricity, so events such as concert parties and movies are not common. There are, however, many traveling movie theaters that tour the villages, carrying their own generators and showing videos and movies. Where there are no clubs, bars, or spare cash, young people gather in village squares at sunset and sing together or play games well into the night. Many villagers have battery-powered radios, but in most small towns there are loudspeaker systems broadcasting radio programs in the streets.

SOCIAL VISITS

Ghanaians enjoy visiting one another's homes. Greetings are very important among them, and even strangers will greet one another in the street. The

Musicians gather at a small rural gathering.

host welcomes his guests with the word *akwaba* (ak-WAH-bah). The guests bring a modest gift of food or even money that will be left discreetly with the woman of the house. The guests are greeted at the entrance, or loggia, of the house, and hands are shaken all around. They are then taken inside and seated. A glass of water is offered, and it is impolite to refuse. Then the host asks the guests why they have come. That is a tradition known as *amanee* (ah-MAH-nee). The family listens while the guests give an account of their journey and reason for coming. Then the host gives a brief recital of recent events in his family, after which he stands again and repeats his welcome. The handshakes are repeated. When that formal part of the visit is finished, everyone relaxes and chats away with a drink of palm wine.

GAMES AND SPORT

By far the most popular sport in Ghana is soccer. Other favorites are boxing, Ping-Pong, hockey, basketball, cricket, and track and field. Ghanaians also play a game similar to cricket called *apaat* (ap-AHT). *Ampe* (AHM-pay), which involves jumping and clapping, is a popular game among Ghanaian girls.

Ghanaian children enjoy playing card games.

Children love to play make-believe, accompanied by songs. Girls usually play apart from boys, but sometimes the children's games bring them together. Traditional games include one similar to checkers; boys' marbles games; and *oware* (oh-WAR-eh), a version of mancala, similar to backgammon, which is played sitting on the ground with a board with small bowls chiseled in it and seeds or pebbles.

MARKET SOCIETY

Buying and selling in the village market is a long, drawn-out, but quite enjoyable process involving much chatting and prolonged bargaining. Buyers mention an item they wish to buy, and the vendor points out the high quality of the item, cost of production, difficulties in transportation, and so on, and names a price. The buyers pretend to be shocked at hearing the price, and so the negotiations begin. When the sale is completed, the buyers may ask for extras. If vegetables

Oware, a version of mancala, is a popular game in Ghana.

Women bargain at a market stall.

were bought, the extras might be salt or cooking spices, or a couple of smaller vegetables to go with the main purchase. The more produce that has been bought, the more the buyer can expect as extras.

In the city, the same process of bargaining takes place over wares in the markets, although extras are usually included only with foodstuffs. In department stores, prices are fixed. Just as in the rest of the world, shopping in department stores or even in markets is often a leisure activity.

INTERNET LINKS

https://broadly.vice.com/en_us/article/bjggyd/in-ghana-women -and-market-queens-dominate-the-economy
This article examines women's role in the market-based economy.

https://www.fifa.com/associations/association=gha/index.html
This page from FIFA, which oversees international soccer, or football, looks at the state of the sport in Ghana.

https://www.timeout.com/accra/things-to-do/best-things-to-do -in-accra-and-ghana-shopping
This *TimeOut* list features 125 things to do in Accra and Ghana.

https://www.youtube.com/watch?v=0nQ3xaKETkg
This video shows activity in Makola Market, one of Ghana's largest.

FESTIVALS

A young Ghanaian man performs a ceremony to honor his ancestors.

12

GHANA HAD THOUSANDS OF YEARS of religious tradition before Christianity and Islam arrived with their own festivals and holidays. Modern Ghana overflows with celebrations. There are over a hundred festivals—regional and tribal, seasonal and commemorative, harvest or historical. Harvest festivals are among the most popular. In a land where drought and famine remain an ongoing threat and subsistence farming is still a way of life for many, the yam harvest is a matter of concern for entire communities, and festivals accompany the harvest.

Other celebrations commemorate the arrival of the clan into Ghana or offer remembrance to the ancestors. Some mark a new start in the year and involve ritual cleaning of the house or clearing of the land around the village. Originally religious in nature, the activities once reaffirmed the group's belief in the spirit world. Today, however, they are more culturally oriented. Celebrations center around the tribal chief—the custodian of the clan's traditions. He has advisers who help him determine the correct date for a festival and the way it should be celebrated.

"The brother or sister who does not respect the traditions of the elders will not be allowed to eat with the elders."

—Ghanaian proverb

The highlight of every festival is the durbar, a kind of pageant, in which the chief of the clan is dressed in his finest clothes and is seated on a palanquin, a chair carried by several of his servants. He is shielded from the heat of the sun by a large and colorful umbrella. The lower chieftains follow in the procession, also adorned in their best clothes. The chiefs are carried to the place where the festival is to take place and their attendants—the executioners of older times—tell stories of past triumphs in battle. Each lesser chief goes before the regional chief to offer his allegiance, taking off his crown and one shoe and bowing before him. The regional chief then makes a welcoming speech to his people, and the festival gets under way.

In the past, urban people were allowed time off from work to return to their ancestral lands to celebrate important festivals. Families would stand at the edge of the village waiting for their relatives in order to escort them home with much music and singing. Anyone who did not take part in the ceremonies could be fined. This rule has been relaxed, as many people now live in the cities and contact with the home village has become less frequent. Nevertheless, the festivals are still a time for returning home if possible, for settling old feuds and land disputes, and for having a very good time. All festivals, even the somber ones, involve a great deal of dancing, singing, feasting, and drinking.

ODWIRA FESTIVAL

Odwira, meaning "purification," is the festival at which the new harvest of yams is presented to the ancestors and rituals are performed to purify the town. This event is celebrated particularly among the Akan people, as well as in Akim, Akuapem, Akwamu, and also other states, though under different names. The celebration itself lasts about a week, but ritual preparations last through an entire *adae* of forty days. It usually takes place in September or October, depending on the harvest. Any eating of new yams is prohibited until the festival is over. For forty days before the festival, all singing, dancing, and noise in the village are banned. Even funerals, which are usually noisy affairs, must be quiet. Seven days before the festival, the path to the mausoleum of the past chiefs is swept.

Six days before, tubers of the new yam harvest are paraded through the streets. A procession goes to the mausoleum with a sheep and rum to feed the spirits of their ancestors. The procession returns to the chief, and a blessing and purification ritual takes place. Drummers triumphantly play all through the night.

On the fifth day before the festival, the village grows silent, and all the local villagers fast and remember their dead ancestors. Everyone wears brown clothes and red turbans to commemorate the dead. On the fourth day before, a huge feast is held for both the living and the dead. Unsalted cooked yam and chicken are taken in procession and laid at a shrine on the outskirts of town. The food for the dead chiefs is placed at the head of the procession, shaded by huge, colorful umbrellas. In every home, food is laid out for everyone to eat, and there is a main feast in the center of the village. That night there is another ceremony, now accompanied by drumming and singing. Most people stay inside their homes as the dead chiefs' stools are paraded through the town to a stream for their annual ceremonial cleansing. Only privileged persons are allowed to see the cherished stools. On the day of the festival is the great durbar, where all the neighboring chiefs arrive to show their respect and pledge their allegiance to the regional chief. They are paraded through the streets of the town, carried on palanquins and accompanied by drummers and servants bearing gold swords and guns. Then the chiefs settle down together in the central square, and dancing and singing performances take place. Drinks and food are offered, and the local chiefs reaffirm their loyalty to the regional chief.

The various clans of the Akan all celebrate different versions of the Odwira festival, but the essential elements are the same—the dead are remembered and thanked for the new yam harvest, the village is purified, the chiefs take part in the durbar, and a great feast is held.

A local tribal chief is honored during the Odwira festival.

OTHER CELEBRATIONS

THE AYERYE This is a Fanti festival in which each newly mature young man of the tribe is initiated into the clan of his father. A boy is a member of his mother's clan until puberty, when he is officially inducted into his father's militia. The festival takes place between September and December, usually to coincide with the harvest festival.

THE ABOAKYIR (DEER HUNT) FESTIVAL In Winneba a three-hundred-year-old festival is held in which two competing teams hunt deer. The winning team is the first one to bring back the game. The trick is that the deer must be brought down with only sticks and cudgels. The festival usually takes place in May.

THE HOMOWO FESTIVAL Among the people of the Ga traditional area in the Accra region, there is a month-long thanksgiving festival that means "hooting at hunger." It originated from a period of great famine that was followed by a bumper harvest of grain and fish. Visitors are invited into village homes to join in the feasting.

THE PATH CLEARING FESTIVAL This festival dates back to the time before modern roads, when it was the duty of each citizen of the village to return home once a year and help clear the village paths, particularly those leading to the shrines and the village well. It is an Akan festival, practiced by the Gomua and Agona tribes.

Nowadays there may be no paths to clear at all, but the festival is still a good reason for families to return home and have some fun together. The festival usually takes place just before the new yams are presented to the ancestors.

INTERNET LINKS

https://www.easytrackghana.com/cultural-overview-ghana_festivals.php
This schedule allows visitors to track upcoming festivals in Ghana.

http://www.ghana.travel/events-festivals
The Ghana Tourism Authority provides a list of festivals and events.

FOOD

Ghanaian food typically is centered on
a starch drenched in sauce.

GHANA IS PART OF WHAT HAS BEEN called the "grain basket" of the African continent. Though Ghana is a poor region for growing wheat, it produces a wide range of other grains, including rice and millet. It is further rich in alternative sources of carbohydrates: bananas and plantains, cassava, African yams, potatoes, and more.

However, Ghana suffers desperate challenges in producing these crops, and in drought-stricken northern regions there has often been famine. Ghanaian food, like many common cuisines, is a peasant cuisine, aiming for reliable calories flavored with generous amounts of seasoning and limited but delicious additions of proteins.

Common Ghanaian dishes are built on a base of starch surrounded by a savory, spicy sauce and gemmed with meats and vegetables. Stomachs are filled and hearts delighted in good times and bad using this formula.

STAPLE FOODS

Staples are the foods that make up the bulk of a person's diet. In the West, that is often wheat, potatoes, or to a lesser extent, rice. In Ghana, the staple foods vary according to the region. In the north, millet (a grain), yams, and corn are the staple foods, while in the south and west, plantains, cassava, and cocoyams (taro) are grown. Across to the southeast, which is drier, corn and cassava are the staple foods. In the center of the country, there are also areas where rice is grown and makes up part of the local diet. Both hill rice and wet rice are grown and eaten in Ghana. Rice is a practical foodstuff because it is easy to store.

Cocoyam grows in the forest regions of Ghana. It is a low-growing plant and needs warm, damp soil. Some cocoyam plants are harvested for the shoots, while others are collected for the roots. An indigenous plant, it grows wild throughout the forested region, but it is also cultivated.

Cassava is a root vegetable that grows in a wide range of conditions, with some species tolerating the dry climate of the north and others preferring the wet forest belt. It is rendered by a complex process into flour. In its raw state, cassava contains a form of cyanide and, if not processed properly, is poisonous. The tubers can be left in the soil until they are needed, and cassava is often the last food staple left at the end of the dry season. Corn and millet are grains that grow in full sun and can tolerate fairly dry conditions. Both the grain and flour are cooked.

MEAT AND FISH

Meat is a rare luxury in many Ghanaians' diet. In rural areas, animals that can be seen and counted by others represent wealth and so are rarely slaughtered. They provide a form of currency and are often used as dowry payments or are bartered at the market for imported goods. When meat does appear in meals, it is usually as an ingredient in a stew rather than as the main dish. Fish and chicken are more common and often appear in stews.

OTHER INGREDIENTS

Groundnuts (peanuts) are an important source of protein and are grown mostly in the north. Palm nuts form the basis of most soups and stews. Other foods include the leaves of the cocoyam, known as *kontomire* (kon-toh-MEER-eh), a form of spinach, and okra, as well as eggplants, onions, tomatoes, sweet potatoes, and many kinds of beans. There are also several vegetables that grow only in specific areas of Ghana and are unknown in other parts.

RURAL KITCHENS

The traditional kitchen in rural houses contains a wood-burning open hearth that is recoated every day in fresh white clay. Standing in the hearth is a tripod for holding the stewpot, while fresh wood is stacked up at the side, ready for use. There is also a covered stove, fueled by charcoal, which is used for faster cooking, such as frying. Assorted pots and pans are stored in a chest. Those often include a big cauldron for cooking stews and a large iron griddle for frying. Out in the yard would be two mortars and pestles—one for crushing small nuts and grains and a larger one for pounding cassava and plantains to make fufu or *kenkey* (ken-KAY).

EVERYDAY MEALS

Usually three meals a day are eaten. In the countryside where there is much work to be done, the midday meal might be only a snack and the breakfast a more substantial meal. In the home, the family separates at mealtimes. The men eat their food from one bowl, taking turns to help themselves with their right hands only. The women and girls share another bowl of food, while the boys eat together. There are well-practiced rules about who eats the meat or fish first and how it is to be shared.

The most commonly eaten evening dish in Ghana is fufu, a dough made from a mixture of cooked cassava and either plantain or cocoyam. It is served with a soup that might be made from a mix of groundnuts, palm fruit, fish, beans, or other vegetables, all simmered for an hour. The soups that include groundnuts are usually thick and grainy, while those made with palm fruit have a thick, yellow, oily texture. Other stews have special names—*forowe* (foh-ROH-weh) is a fish stew with tomatoes, while *nkatekwan* (en-KATI-ku-an) is a chicken and peanut stew.

Chilies are commonly grown and used in Ghanaian cooking, and a favorite soup is pepper soup, which is hot and peppery.

A popular breakfast dish called *ampesi* (am-PEH-si) consists of cassava, cocoyam, yam, and plantain mixed together, boiled, pounded to break up the fibers, and then boiled again with onion and fish.

Another common base for a meal is kenkey, which is made from cornmeal. The meal is ground and soaked in water and left to ferment for two days. Then the mash is formed into balls and dropped into boiling water. After an hour, the pasty mash balls are wrapped in plantain-leaf packages and kept for two days. They are eaten with a spicy sauce with fish or stew as a substitute for fufu. Similar fermented dough is made from cornmeal or millet in the north of the country. The Ewe make a version from corn dough and cassava mash.

SWEETS

There are many sweet dishes in Ghana. Surprisingly, though, not many of them are made from chocolate, despite the fact that chocolate is cheap and of very good quality in Ghana. Some sweet dishes are built around the staple starchy vegetables. One popular dish is *tartare* (TAR-tar), or pancakes made from ripe plantain, pounded and deep-fried in palm oil. Mixed with corn flour and made into balls like doughnut "holes," plantain becomes *krako* (KRAH-koe). With boiled soybeans added, it becomes *aboboe* (ah-BO-bo-ee). Sweet dishes are not served as desserts after the main course, but are eaten as snacks at any time of the day.

RESTAURANTS AND STREET FOOD

As Ghana has a growing tourist industry, there are many restaurants that cater both to foreigners and to wealthier Ghanaians, especially in towns along the southern coast. Foreign cuisine, especially European-style, Indian, and Chinese, is common. Less expensive are the chop houses, which are casual cafés selling local food. The cheapest way of eating out is at a street stall, usually run by a woman, selling rice with various toppings. A popular street snack is *kelewele* (ke-leh-WEH-leh), or fried plantains seasoned with ginger and chili. *Koko* (KO-ko) is corn or millet porridge mixed with milk and sugar. Other stalls sell slices of fresh fruit or coconuts that are slashed open on the spot for the customer to enjoy the water and meat.

BEVERAGES

As readily available in Ghana as in the rest of the world are the ubiquitous cola drinks. Ghana produces some soft drinks of its own, such as Refresh, a fizzy soda made with fresh fruit juice, and Supermalt, a dark-colored nonalcoholic drink tasting of malt. Beer is very popular. Ghana was the first West African country to have a brewery. There are several local beers nowadays, as well as imported beers. More unusual drinks include iced kenkey, which is the northern fermented corn flour dissolved in water and fermented further. Another unusual taste more common in the north is *pito* (PEE-toh) beer, made from millet rather than hops. In the south, the drink of choice is palm wine, which can range from very alcoholic to nearly nonalcoholic.

INTERNET LINKS

http://ghananet.weebly.com/ghana-food-and-drink.html
This article on *Ghana Net* examines traditional Ghanaian food and drink.

https://www.independent.co.uk/life-style/food-and-drink/zoe -adjonyo-ghana-heatlhy-diet-chef-african-food-myth-lack-training -cooking-recipes-a7766876.html
This article by Zoe Adjonyoh examines the healthy Ghanaian diet.

https://theculturetrip.com/africa/ghana/articles/10-traditional -ghanaian-dishes-you-need-to-try
Culture Trip provides a list of ten traditional Ghanaian dishes to try.

RED RED (BLACK-EYED PEA STEW)

The name "red red" comes from the tomato that colors the finished stew. This is a dish that can be varied in many ways, and made vegan, vegetarian, or meat-enhanced without betraying the soul of the dish. A regional basic, as common and loved as American meatloaf or spaghetti, it has millions of variations.

1 pound (0.5 kilograms) dried
  black-eyed peas
1 inch (2.5 centimeters) fresh ginger,
  grated
3—4 cloves fresh garlic, chopped
1 large onion, chopped
1 28-ounce (794-gram) can of
  diced tomatoes
2 tablespoons tomato paste
Hot pepper (habanero, Scotch bonnet,
  or other fierce chili) to taste
Pinch of sugar
Salt to taste

Soak black-eyed peas 1—4 hours, then drain and simmer until done. Drain, reserving cooking liquid.

Sauté ginger, garlic, and onion until turning golden-brown. Add tomatoes and tomato paste and then thin with some of the cooking fluid. Add sugar, salt, and hot pepper. Allow to boil for 30 minutes.

Add black-eyed peas and bring to a boil again. Once it boils, turn down the heat and let it simmer for 15 minutes. If you wish to thicken the soup, mash some of the peas and simmer to reduce liquid.

(Note: If you are wary of hot peppers, consider using a chili sauce instead. Tabasco and sriracha sauce are not authentic, but they are still based on chilies, and they're easier to control.)

JOLLOF RICE

3—4 large Roma tomatoes, diced

½ fresh hot pepper (Scotch bonnet, cayenne, jalapeño—hotter is authentic, less hot is safer for those unfamiliar with spice)

2 red onions, sliced thin

4 large cloves of garlic, pressed or minced

2 red bell peppers, sliced

1 to 3 teaspoons curry powder to taste, brand of your choice

2 bay leaves, broken up

1 tablespoon thyme

3 cups (600 grams) medium-grain rice

Sauté the hot pepper, red onions, and garlic on medium burner until golden brown.

Add red peppers, sauté until just soft.

Add tomatoes, curry powder, bay leaf, and thyme.

Add 3 cups of rice, and water to cover. Raise liquid to a gentle boil.

Cover the pan and turn the burner to the lowest setting. Be very careful the rice does not burn. The heat should be very low, barely enough to keep the pan hot

Let sit 20 minutes, then open and serve.

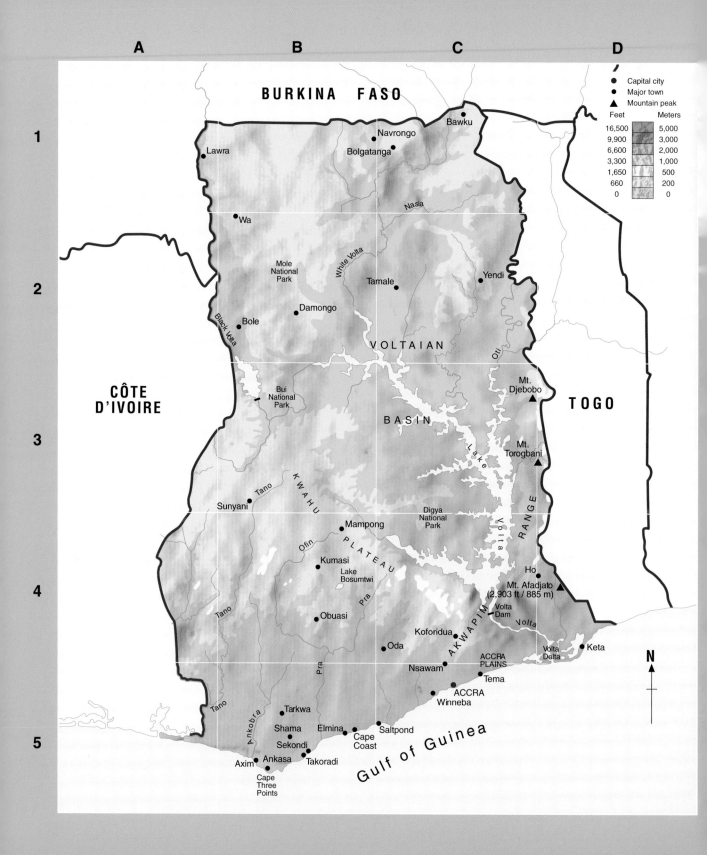

MAP OF GHANA

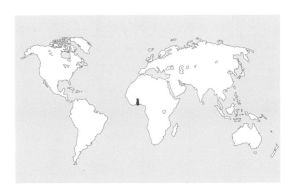

ECONOMIC GHANA

Services

 Airports

 Ports

 Tourism

Manufacturing

 Chemicals

 Food and beverages

 Furniture

 Textiles

Agriculture

 Cacao

 Cashew nuts

 Cola nuts

 Cotton

 Palm

 Shea nuts

 Timber

 Tobacco

Natural Resources

 Fishing

 Gold

 Hydroelectric power

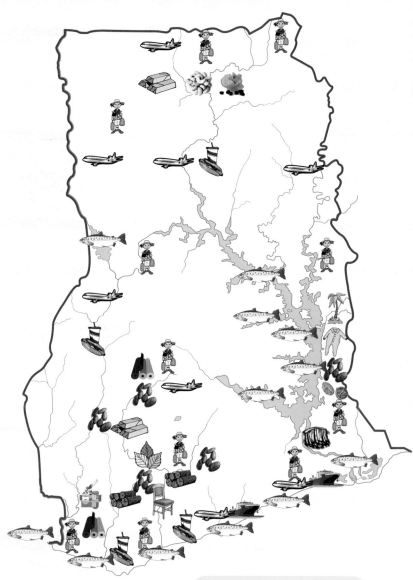

ABOUT THE ECONOMY

OVERVIEW

Ghana is well endowed with natural resources of gold and is a world producer of cacao. Many Ghanaians, 44 percent of the workforce, are employed in agriculture. Gold, cacao, and timber are major sources of foreign exchange. Ghanaians aspire to achieve economic success by creating a favorable business environment. With some international financial aid and technical assistance, Ghana may one day soon realize its vision, given the tenacity of its people to succeed.

GROSS DOMESTIC PRODUCT (GDP)

$45.46 billion (2017 estimate)

GDP GROWTH

5.9 percent (2017 estimate)

INFLATION RATE

11.8 percent (2017 estimate)

POPULATION BELOW POVERTY LINE

24.2 percent (2013 estimate)

CURRENCY

The cedi (GHS)
1 cedi = 100 pesewas
Notes: 1, 5, 10, 20, and 50 cedis
Coins: 1, 5, 10, 20, and 50 pesewas, and 1 cedi
USD 1 = 4.42 cedis (2018 estimate)

LABOR FORCE

12.49 million (2015 estimate)

UNEMPLOYMENT RATE

11.9 percent (2015 estimate)

AGRICULTURAL PRODUCTS

Cacao, rice, cassava (tapioca), peanuts, corn, shea nuts, bananas, timber

NATURAL RESOURCES

Gold, timber, industrial diamonds, bauxite, manganese, fish, rubber, hydropower, salt, petroleum, silver, limestone

MAIN INDUSTRIES

Mining, lumbering, light manufacturing, aluminum smelting, food processing, cement, small commercial ship building

MAIN EXPORTS

Gold, cacao, timber, tuna, bauxite, aluminum, manganese ore, diamonds, horticulture

MAIN IMPORTS

Capital equipment, petroleum, foodstuffs

MAIN TRADE PARTNERS

Export partners: Switzerland, 17.6 percent; India, 14.7 percent; United Arab Emirates, 13.4 percent; China, 8.9 percent; Vietnam, 5.2 percent; Netherlands, 4.2 percent; Burkina Faso, 4 percent
Import partners: China, 17.3 percent; United Kingdom, 9.7 percent; United States, 7.7 percent; Belgium, 5.1 percent; India, 4.6 percent.

CULTURAL GHANA

Navrongo Cathedral
Built in 1906 and originally called Our Lady of Seven Sorrows, this traditionally built structure was painstakingly constructed and decorated by the locals, and is also the last remaining mud cathedral in Ghana.

Wechiau Hippo Sanctuary
This 25-mile- (40 km) long and 1-mile- (1.6 km) wide sanctuary stretches down the length of the Black Volta River, and is home to various species of mammals and reptiles. Besides the many trails to explore, hikers can also spend the night in jungle treehouses and experience one of the best dawn choruses of bird song in all of Africa.

Larabanga Mosque
Considered one of the most endangered monuments worldwide, this thirteenth-century historic Sudanese mosque is one of the holiest sites in Ghana. An ancient Quran believed to have descended from heaven is still preserved in this architecturally marvelous mosque.

Boabeng-Fiema Monkey Sanctuary
This unique sanctuary is the only place where two different species of monkeys, the Campbell's mona and the Geoffroy's colobus, live harmoniously together alongside human beings. Regarded as sacred, protected by the law, and given proper funerals, these monkeys are part of society, and local culture has been fashioned to include their acceptance.

Kakum National Park
Located in Elmina, Africa's only canopy walkway is suspended 100 feet (30.5 m) from the ground, offering a spectacular view from the tallest trees and a colorful array of patterns as the tropical birds glide through the lush greenery of the rain forest below.

Cape Coast Castle
This fortified castle and UNESCO heritage site was originally built by the Swedes in 1653 for the gold trade. Later seized by the Danes and then conquered by the British, the castle was used as a main slave-trading fort during the transatlantic slave trade.

Kwame Nkrumah National Park
Located in the main commercial area in Accra, the structures in this park provide interesting symbolic interpretations of the life and works of Dr. Nkrumah, widely regarded as the "founding father" of Ghana.

Volta Dam
The construction of this hydroelectric dam flooded the Volta River Basin and subsequently created Lake Volta, one of the world's largest man-made lake.

ABOUT THE CULTURE

OFFICIAL NAME
Republic of Ghana

TOTAL AREA
92,098 square miles (238,533 sq km)

CAPITAL
Accra

ADMINISTRATIVE DIVISIONS
Ashanti, Brong-Ahafo, Central, Eastern, Greater Accra, Northern, Upper East, Upper West, Volta, Western

HIGHEST POINT
Mount Afadjato (2,903 feet/885 m)

POPULATION
27.5 million (2017 estimate)

LIFE EXPECTANCY
Total population: 67 years
Male: 64.5 years
Female: 69.6 years (2017 estimate)

LITERACY RATE
76.6 percent (2015 estimate)

BIRTHRATE
30.5 births per 1,000 population
(2017 estimate)

ETHNIC GROUPS
Akan, 47.5 percent; Dagomba, 16.6 percent; Ewe, 13.9 percent; Ga-Dangme, 7.4 percent; Gurma, 5.7 percent; Guan, 3.7 percent; Grusi, 2.5 percent; Mande, 1.1 percent; other tribes, 1.4 percent.

RELIGION
Christianity, 71.2 percent; Islam, 17.6 percent; traditional African beliefs, 5.2 percent.

LANGUAGES
English is the official language; Ashanti, 16 percent; Ewe, 14 percent; Fanti, 11.6 percent; Boron (Brong), 4.9 percent; Dagboni, 4.4 percent; Dangme, 4.2 percent; Dagarte (Dagaba), 3.9 percent; Kokomba, 3.5 percent; Akyem, 3.2 percent; Ga, 3.1 percent; other, 31.2 percent

NATIONAL HOLIDAYS
New Year (January 1); Independence Day (March 6); Good Friday (variable); Easter (variable); Labor Day (May 1); Africa Day (May 25); Republic Day (July 1); Eid al-Fitr, or End of Ramadan (variable); National Farmers' Day (first Friday of December); Eid al-Adha, or Feast of the Sacrifice (variable); Christmas (December 25/26); Revolution Day (December 31)

TIMELINE

IN GHANA	IN THE WORLD

5500–2500 BCE
Hunter-gatherer communities are formed in the plains around Ghana.

600 CE
Height of Mayan civilization

1200 CE
The Akan people's kingdom grows in Ghana's northern grasslands.

1206–1368
Genghis Khan unifies the Mongols and starts conquest of the world. At its height, the Mongol Empire under Kublai Khan stretches from China to Persia and parts of Europe and Russia.

1471
Portuguese traders arrive near Elmina.

1481
Portuguese mission led by Diogo d'Azambuja discovers gold in Volta plains.

1492
Christopher Columbus sets foot in America.

1500
The Ga and Adangme tribes settle around Accra.

1598
The Dutch build forts along Ghana's coastal area to secure trade.

1664
Britain establishes headquarters at Cape Coast Castle.

1776
US Declaration of Independence.

1874
Britain makes the Gold Coast a crown colony.

1925
First legislative council elections take place.

1939
World War II begins.

1952
Kwame Nkrumah is designated prime minister of the British colony's first African government.

1957
Ghana, with Kwame Nkrumah as prime minister, gains its independence from the British Empire. It is the first sub-Saharan African country to become independent.

1957
The Russians launch *Sputnik*.

1960
Ghana is proclaimed a republic. Nkrumah is elected president of Ghana.

1969
A new constitution facilitates transfer of power to a civilian government led by Kofi Busia.

1969
Apollo 11 lands the first men on the moon.

1975
The Khmer Rouge ruthlessly rules Cambodia, led by despot Pol Pot.

IN GHANA	IN THE WORLD

1979
Jerry Rawlings leads a coup overthrowing the government. He steps down soon after

1981
Rawlings leads a second coup and stays in power.

1992
Rawlings is elected president. A new constitution introduces a multiparty system.

1994
Ethnic clashes erupt in northern Ghana between the Konkomba and the Nanumba

1996
Jerry Rawlings is reelected president.

2001
John Kofi Agyekum Kufuor is elected president. He serves until 2009.

2002
President Kufuor appoints reconciliation commission to look into human rights violations during military rule.

2005
Thousands of Togolese refugees fleeing political violence arrive in Ghana.

2008
Professor John Evans Atta Mills is elected president.

2009
The International Monetary Fund gives Ghana a three-year loan for $600 million to revive its economy.

2012
Communal violence erupts over the disinterment of a Muslim cleric.

2017
Ghanaians celebrate the sixtieth anniversary of independence.

2018
Ghana's economy takes a global lead and becomes one of the fastest growing economies in the world.

1991
Breakup of the Soviet Union

2001
Terrorists crash planes in New York, Washington, DC, and Pennsylvania, on September 11.

2003
The War in Iraq begins.

2016
Great Britain votes to exit the European Union.

2017
Donald Trump becomes US president.

2018
The Winter Olympics take place in Pyeongchang, South Korea.

GLOSSARY

abosom (ah-BOH-som)
Akan name for an animist spirit.

abusa (ah-BOO-sah)
Clan or family grouping.

adae (AHD-ay)
A period of forty days in the Akan calendar.

akpeteshe (ak-pet-ESH-ee)
Distilled palm wine.

akwaba (ak-WAH-bah)
A Ghanaian word of welcome.

amanee (ah-MAH-nee)
Custom of asking and explaining reasons for a home visit.

apaat (ap-AHT)
A game similar to cricket.

apirede (ap-eer-EH-deh)
A traditional orchestral ensemble consisting of drums, a gong, and clappers, played by ceremonial Ashanti stool carriers.

atumpan (at-UM-pan)
Talking drum of the Akan.

durbar
Pageant during a festival.

enstoolment
The ceremony of enthroning a new chief.

fetish house
A building dedicated to an animist spirit.

fufu (FOO-foo)
A staple food made from pounded cassava and either plantain or cocoyam.

highlife
Ghanaian style of music that blends Western and African influences.

juju
A form of folk medicine practiced by animist priests.

kente cloth
Traditional Ashanti cloth, woven in colorful strips and sewn together to make clothing.

malam
A Muslim religious healer in Ghana.

okyeame (otch-ee-AH-mee)
Linguist who accompanies the chief.

oware (oh-WAR-eh)
Traditional variant of mancala, somewhat like backgammon, played on the ground with seeds or pebbles.

pito (PEE-toh)
A beer brewed from millet.

FOR FURTHER INFORMATION

BOOKS

Briggs, Philip. *Ghana*. London, UK: Bradt Travel Guides, 2017.

International Monetary Fund. *Ghana*. Washington, DC: International Monetary Fund, 2015.

Utley, Ian. *Ghana*. London, UK: Kuperard, 2016.

FILMS

Adom-Otchere, Paul. *From Gold Coast to Ghana: A Glorious History of Self Determination*, 2017.

Anas, Anas Aremeyaw. *Ghana in the Eyes of God: Epic of Injustice*, 2010.

Wendl, Tobias, and Nancy du Plessis. *Future Remembrance: Photography and Image Arts in Ghana,* 1998.

MUSIC

Asante Kete Drumming: Music of Ghana, Lyrichord Discs Inc., 2007.

Black Stars: Ghana's Hiplife Generation, Out Here Records, 2008.

Highlife Time 2: Nigerian and Ghanaian Classics, Vampisoul, 2011.

Obo Addy and Kukrudu, *Let Me Play My Drums,* CD Baby, 2016.

Por Por: Honk Horn Music of Ghana, Smithsonian Folkways, 2007.

Soundway Presents Ghana Special: Modern Highlife, Afro Sounds & Ghanaian Blues, 1968—81, Soundway Records, 2012.

BIBLIOGRAPHY

BOOKS

Edgerton, Robert B. *The Fall of the Asante Empire: The Hundred-Year War for Africa's Gold Coast.* New York: The Free Press, 1995.

Hadjor, Kofi Buenor. *Nkrumah and Ghana.* London, UK: Kegan Paul International, 1988.

Ray, Donald Iain. *Ghana: Politics, Economics, and Society.* Marxist Regimes Series. Boulder, CO: L. Rienner Publishers, 1986.

Trillo, Richard, and Jim Hudgens. *The Rough Guide to West Africa.* New York: The Rough Guides Publisher, 2009.

WEBSITES

Central Intelligence Agency World Factbook. https://www.cia.gov/library/publications/resources/the-world-factbook/index.html.

"Ghana." *Food in Every Country.* http://www.foodbycountry.com/Germany-to-Japan/Ghana.html.

GhanaWeb. https://www.ghanaweb.com.

Government of Ghana. http://www.ghana.gov.gh.

"High-Tech Trash." *National Geographic.* http://ngm.nationalgeographic.com/print/2008/01/high-tech-trash/carroll-text.

"Moving Up from Akosombo." *International Water Power and Dam Construction.* http://www.waterpowermagazine.com/news/newsmoving-up-from-akosombo.

Touring Ghana. http://www.touringghana.com.

INDEX